HOW BANKS TREAT FOREIGN EXCHANGE IN MULTI-CURRENCY ACCOUNTING

HOW BANKS TREAT FX IN MULTI-CURRENCY ACCOUNTING

First edition. May 19, 2023.

ISBN: 979-8215086773

Written by Pat Low.

Table of Contents

To my lovely wife Miriam. Thank you for your patience and understanding whilst I invested time and effort into this project which is my maiden attempt at writing a book.

1. Introduction

Transacting in various currencies and the need to record in a particular currency presents bookkeeping issues because of exchange rate fluctuations. Traditionally, the home or domestic currency is used as the unit of account, often called the base currency. All other currencies are foreign currencies and any transactions denominated in them need to be converted to the base currency to be captured in the accounts. Over time, historical cost and fair value concepts have evolved and accounting standards have been established on how to treat foreign currency transactions.

This may surprise some. For banks, there is no foreign currency in the accounting sense. It sounds oxymoronic but walk through the explanatory debits and credits in 1he book, it becomes apparent.

For banks, dealing in a particular currency in and of itself, does not present any exchange risk given exchange rate fluctuations. For example, extending a YEN loan, accepting CHF deposits, investing in AUD corporate bonds, etc., such transactions present no exchange risks per se. Banks view spot risks as the mismatch between a currency's assets and liabilities. These are currency positions created by foreign exchange transactions, i.e., banks' buying and selling of currencies. Banks' forward currency risks are associated with their portfolio of foreign exchange carry trades. The values of these spot cash positions and carry trades are subject to exchange rate volatility.

Bank accounting efforts are directed towards providing fair value for spot currency positions, mark-to-market of carry trades, and realisation values of delivered trades. This book shows how this is done in a multi-currency accounting system. In addition, it also shows technicalities of multi-currency systems is an elephant in the room not addressed by international accounting standards.

This is a primer on the bookkeeping aspects of foreign exchange transactions in a multi-currency system. It is written for middle office personnel in banks, central bank inspectors, bank internal auditors, public accountants handling a banking portfolio, or accounting professionals and students who want to learn a subject matter hardly covered in text books or reference materials, and the general public who want some heady stuff demystified for them.

****

2. Accounting Standards for foreign currency transactions

Companies maintain a set of accounts to record all transactions. The recording is done in a single currency called 'base' currency. The term 'base' is not to be confused as that used by FX traders which is an identifier in a currency pair (explained in chap.7). To be clear, let's call this the book currency. The book currency in a single currency accounting system is usually the home (domestic) currency. A company may choose to use a different currency to record transactions if their major economic activity is in that currency. That is known as the functional currency. In other words, a book currency can be either the domestic currency or the functional currency. All other currencies are then considered 'foreign' currencies. Should a company in Singapore use USD as its functional currency, then the domestic SGD is treated as a foreign currency.

Accounting standards are established on how to record foreign currency transactions at inception, on their impact on profit and loss during their life, and on disposal.

Basically, in single currency systems, all foreign currency transactions are recognised and recorded in the books in the base currency using temporal or historical method, i.e., based on rates at the date of transactions.

Various foreign currency monetary and non- assets and liabilities are revalued for year end reporting and exchange gains and losses recognised by translating at rates on year end dates. Finally, on settlement or disposal they are valued on rates at maturity or disposal date and gains or losses on exchange recognised.

Illustration:

A company whose book currency is SGD, exported some products invoiced on 1 Oct 2021 for USD100,000. The customer eventually paid up on 15 February 2022. Exchange rates on relevant dates were :

- 1 Oct 2021 1.3580
- 31 Oct 2021 1.3500
- 31 Dec 2021 1.3487
- 15 Feb 2022 1.3465

The relevant accounting entries:

VR2-1		Ccy	Dr	Cr	
	SGD LEDGER : Accounts				
10 Oct 2021	Trade debtors	SGD	135,800		(1)
	Sales	SGD		135,800	
31 Dec 2021	Exchange p&l	SGD	930		(2)
	Provision - translation	SGD		930	
15 Fed 2022	Cash	SGD	134,650		(3)
	Trade Debtors	SGD		135,800	
	Provision-translation	SGD	930		
	Exchange p&l	SGD	220		

- (1) USD100,000x1.3580 = SGD135,800 based on rate on date of transaction.
- (2) To record loss in value of trade debt :
  USD100,000x1.3487 = SGD134,870.
  SGD135,800-SGD134,870 = SGD930.
- (3) To record loss in value on settlement :
  USD100,000x1.3465 = SGD134,650.
  Realised loss is : SGD135,800-SGD134,650=SGD1,150.

The financial reporting as at 31 Dec 2021 :

Sales USD100,000 x 1.3500 = SGD135,000
Debtors USD100,000 x 1.3487 = SGD134,870
Provision for loss = SGD 930

This serves the purpose for most businesses.

Entities consolidating foreign operations:

Some companies may have overseas branches, joint-ventures, subsidiaries etc. These overseas operations submit financial returns in a different presentation currency. To consolidate the accounts, the parent company translates by:

- Assets and Liabilities at year end rates.
- Revenue and Expenses at rate on date of transaction. If this is not possible, average rates are used.

Take an example of a US company working on its Australian branch financials.

Tab2-1 US Parent Company with Australian Branch

				Monthly Profit			MTD Profit	
				@ Month	@ Average		@ Month	@ Average
Mth	Ledger	Rate		Rate	Rate	Ledger	Rate	Rate
	AUD	Month end	Average	USD	USD	AUD	USD	USD
1	240,000	1.2000	1.1700	200,000	205,128	240,000	200,000	205,128
2	270,500	1.2050	1.1750	224,481	230,213	510,500	423,651	435,341
3	420,500	1.2150	1.1880	346,091	353,956	931,000	766,255	789,297
4	470,445	1.2450	1.2380	377,867	380,004	1,401,445	1,125,659	1,169,301
5	455,000	1.2500	1.2485	364,000	364,437	1,856,445	1,485,156	1,533,739
6	505,000	1.3000	1.2700	388,462	397,638	2,361,445	1,816,496	1,931,376
7	560,220	1.3800	1.3680	405,957	409,518	2,921,665	2,117,149	2,340,894
8	540,200	1.4200	1.3885	380,423	389,053	3,461,865	2,437,933	2,729,947
9	500,700	1.4250	1.4225	351,368	351,986	3,962,565	2,780,747	3,081,933
10	560,705	1.4400	1.4377	389,378	390,001	4,523,270	3,141,160	3,471,934
11	460,700	1.4700	1.4600	313,401	315,548	4,983,970	3,390,456	3,787,482
12	470,800	1.5000	1.4850	313,867	317,037	5,454,770	3,636,513	4,104,519
Total	5,454,770			4,055,295	4,104,519			
	1.5000							
USD	3,636,513			(1)	(2)		(3)	(4)

1. AUD balances translated at month end rate.
2. AUD translated at the monthly average rates per IAS21.
3. AUD cumulative balances translated at the rate of the reporting month end. Thus on month end 12 the year-to-date profit in USD is the total AUD5,454,770 translated at 1.5000 = USD3,636,513.
4. Cumulative of monthly AUD translated at each month's average rate. Note the anomaly of monthly USD aggregate of USD4,055,295 compared to cumulative figure of SD3,636,513.

To comply with accounting standards means a manual post year-end adjustment of USD468,006 (4,104,519 - 3,636,513) is required for exchange gains on translation :

- Credit Profit & Loss A/C
- Debit Reserves A/C

It is clear when rates are volatile sideways, the translation differences may even out over time. But in the case where there is prolonged period of appreciation or depreciation of a currency, there will be significant translation impact on p&l. In the illustration above, the huge exchange gains on translation is a reflection of AUD on a long stretch of depreciation against USD.

****

3. Why banks are different

Currency is a stock-in-trade for banks. Buying and selling currencies is a major part of their business. Currency is a commodity and their approach to accounting is basically that of a trader. They see value changes in open currency positions and seek some means of valuation to recognise daily gains or losses.

Banks maintain multi-currency accounting systems, with a self-balancing ledger for each currency they do business in. In a multi-currency accounting system, each currency is a home currency in its own ledger. All transactions are recognised and recorded in the relevant currency ledger. There is thus no 'foreign currency' in the traditional sense.

Any transaction involving only one currency does not cause an exchange difference. It merely causes a compensating movement in the assets and liabilities of the relevant currency ledger. For example, a bank in Singapore receives EUR to place on a term deposit. Its EUR Nostro balance increases and a customer's EUR term deposit account is set up. When the deposit matures, the customer withdraws the currency. The bank sees their EUR Nostro balance decline, and their EUR deposit liability vanishes. The transaction is recorded exclusively in the EUR ledger. As no exchange is involved, no exchange gains or losses occur.

In a multi-currency system, exchange gains or losses arise only in transactions involving currency exchange. This is predominantly in the form of foreign exchange trades where banks buy and sell one currency for another. When an investor buys some shares in the stock exchange, he has an exposure in a particular company. In FX trading, each currency pair is a product. When a bank writes an FX deal, it has an exposure in the relevant currency pair traded. Banks hold large exposures in various pairs of currencies in their carry trades, i.e., all outstanding forward-dated FX deals.

The huge volume of FX trades in banks come from 3 main areas – servicing customers' needs, internal hedging activities, and speculation or position taking by the trading desk. Banks monitor these carry trade exposures and compute unrealised exchange gains and losses on a daily basis.

The value of such trades changes as the exchange rate changes. Banks track the impact of changing exchange rates through FX trade life cycle. Thus banks perform revaluation of outstanding FX contracts to determine unrealised exchange gains or losses, and on matured FX deals to determine realised exchange gains or losses.

Banks perform another form of daily revaluation exercise. As FX deals reach a value date, they are settled. Banks receive in one currency, and pay out in another currency. This creates an asset-liability mismatch in both currency ledgers. For accounting purposes, a spot exchange position account is maintained in each currency ledger to balance double-entry bookkeeping. Spot exchange position accounts are 'mirror' or compensating accounts that get eliminated in a consolidated reporting currency. Spot exchange positions reflect a bank's mismatch in a relevant currency, i.e., when the bank has net assets (a long position) or net liabilities (a short position). In a multi-currency system, a balance in the spot exchange position account means the bank has an open spot position in that currency. The value of an open spot position changes with changing exchange rates. Thus banks revalue their spot (or cash) positions daily. IAS21 does not address this.

Since the currency ledgers are self-balanced, translation and consolidation into any reporting or presentation currency at any time will never cause exchange gains or losses if (a) there are no open currency positions, and (b) if there are open positions, they have been revalued. The currency ledgers are consolidated in a reporting currency by the 'current' method, i.e., using the rate on the reporting date.

All these will be fully explained with illustrations in following chapters.

****

4. No foreign currency transaction gains or losses in banks

Let's be more precise about what is meant by foreign exchange (FX) transactions and foreign currency transactions in the context of his book.

FX transactions pertain to currency buying and selling. Foreign currency transactions pertain to the recording of an economic activity that involves a currency which is not the currency of account. For example, a company in Singapore may use domestic SGD to keep account, or it may use a functional currency such as USD. If it uses USD to keep account, then doing business in any other currency is considered a foreign currency transaction, including SGD.

In a single currency accounting system, all foreign currency transactions are booked at the rate on the date of the transaction. If they involve assets or liabilities, they are revalued for financial reporting based on the rate on the report date. Losses from currency revaluation are taken into account and the asset or liability balances adjusted for the current value. On disposal, the assets or liabilities are revalued at the rate on the date of disposal. The difference is reflected in the accounts as realised exchange gains or losses.

In a multi-currency system, a separate and self-balancing set of ledgers is opened for each currency the bank deals in. In other words, each currency is its own book currency. All transactions, whether they involve assets, liabilities, revenue or expenses, are recorded in the relevant currency ledgers. There is then no such thing as foreign currency in such a system, and no exchange gains or losses arise when dealing with foreign currency transactions.

Suppose a bank in Singapore has assets and liabilities like this:

Fig.1 Multi-currency Assets-Liabilities status

	USD Ledger		SGD Ledger		AUD Ledger		Reporting SGD	
	Assets	Liabilities	Assets	Liabilities	Assets	Liabilities	Assets	Liabilities
Equity	0	0	0	1,005,000	0	0	0	1,005,000
Deposits from banks	0	2,500,000	0	550,000	0	100,000	0	3,895,000
Customer deposits	0	750,000	0	2,000,000	0	20,000	0	2,994,000
Loans	3,000,000	0	2,350,000	0	0	0	6,250,000	0
Deposits with banks	200,000	0	1,200,000	0	110,000	0	1,564,500	0
Investments	0	0	0	0	0	0	0	0
Others	55,000	5,000	30,000	25,000	10,000	0	111,000	31,500
TOTAL	3,255,000	3,255,000	3,580,000	3,580,000	120,000	120,000	7,925,500	7,925,500
Book rates	1.3000	1.3000	1.0000	1.0000	0.9500	0.9500		
Translated to SGD	4,231,500	4,231,500	3,580,000	3,580,000	114,000	114,000	7,925,500	7,925,500

Suppose the USD3,000,000 loan matured. The borrower repays and the bank uses half of it to buy USD bonds, the other half it places in the money market with other banks.

Fig.2 Multi-currency Assets-Liabilities after currency transaction

	USD Ledger		SGD Ledger		AUD Ledger		Reporting SGD	
	Assets	Liabilities	Assets	Liabilities	Assets	Liabilities	Assets	Liabilities
Equity				1,005,000			0	1,005,000
Deposits from banks		2,500,000		550,000		100,000	0	4,019,000
Customer deposits		750,000		2,000,000		20,000	0	3,031,300
Loans			2,350,000				2,350,000	0
Deposits with banks	1,700,000		1,200,000		110,000		3,598,400	0
Investments	1,500,000						2,025,000	0
Others	55,000	5,000	30,000	25,000	10,000		113,650	31,750
TOTAL	3,255,000	3,255,000	3,580,000	3,580,000	120,000	120,000	8,087,050	8,087,050
Book rates	1.3500	1.3500	1.0000	1.0000	0.9400	0.9400		
Translated to SGD	4,394,250	4,394,250	3,580,000	3,580,000	112,800	112,800	8,087,050	8,087,050

A transaction that involves only one currency simply results in some compensating movements in the relevant currency ledger. It does not result in any foreign exchange gains or losses. This is even though the rates have changed.

****

5. No translation gains or losses for financial reporting by banks

And the reason is banks maintain multi-currency accounting systems with a separate ledger for each currency

It may surprise most. Banks do not report translation gains or losses when the various currency ledgers are consolidated in a presentation currency. In a multi-currency system, each currency ledger self-balances. Inter-currency transactions are facilitated by the use of spot exchange position accounts which are mirror or compensating mechanisms to balance assets-liabilities mismatch in the individual currency ledgers. These exchange position accounts are eliminated when the books are consolidated into a presentation or reporting currency on any date.

Suppose the currency ledger balances are :

Fig-3 Multi-currency Assets-Liabilities

	USD Ledger		SGD Ledger		AUD Ledger	
	Assets	Liabilities	Assets	Liabilities	Assets	Liabilities
Other assets-liabilities	5,155,000	5,000,000	325,000	460,000	219,150	300,000
Spot exchange position	0	155,000	135,000	0	80,850	0
TOTAL	5,155,000	5,155,000	460,000	460,000	300,000	300,000

The exchange rates are USD/SGD - 1.3500. USD/AUD -1.4700, & AUD/SGD 0.9184.

For financial reporting purposes, a currency consolidated report in USD is required.

Fig-4 Multi-currency Assets-Liabilities presented in USD

	USD Ledger		SGD Ledger		AUD Ledger		Reporting USD	
	Assets	Liabilities	Assets	Liabilities	Assets	Liabilities	Assets	Liabilities
Other assets-liabilities	5,155,000	5,000,000	325,000	460,000	219,150	300,000	5,544,822	5,544,822
Spot exchange position	0	155,000	135,000	0	80,850	0	155,000	155,000
TOTAL	5,155,000	5,155,000	460,000	460,000	300,000	300,000	5,699,822	5,699,822
Book rates	1.0000	1.0000	1.3500	1.3500	1.4700	1.4700		
Translated to USD	5,155,000	5,155,000	340,741	340,741	204,082	204,082	5,699,822	5,699,822

What if it's translated to AUD?

Fig-5 Multi-currency Assets-Liabilities presented in AUD

	USD Ledger		SGD Ledger		AUD Ledger		Reporting AUD	
	Assets	Liabilities	Assets	Liabilities	Assets	Liabilities	Assets	Liabilities
Other assets-liabilities	5,155,000	5,000,000	325,000	460,000	219,150	300,000	8,150,889	8,150,889
Spot exchange position	0	155,000	135,000	0	80,850	0	227,850	227,850
TOTAL	5,155,000	5,155,000	460,000	460,000	300,000	300,000	8,378,739	8,378,739
Book rates	1.4700	1.4700	0.9183673	0.9183673	1.0000	1.0000		
Translated to AUD	7,577,850	7,577,850	500,889	500,889	300,000	300,000	8,378,739	8,378,739

How about in SGD?

Fig-6 Multi-currency Assets-Liabilities presented in SGD

	USD Ledger		SGD Ledger		AUD Ledger		Reporting SGD	
	Assets	Liabilities	Assets	Liabilities	Assets	Liabilities	Assets	Liabilities
Other assets-liabilities	5,155,000	5,000,000	325,000	460,000	219,150	300,000	7,485,510	7,485,510
Spot exchange position	0	155,000	135,000	0	80,850	0	209,250	209,250
TOTAL	5,155,000	5,155,000	460,000	460,000	300,000	300,000	7,694,760	7,694,760
Book rates	1.3500	1.3500	1.0000	1.0000	0.9183673	0.9183673		
Translated to SGD	6,959,250	6,959,250	460,000	460,000	275,510	275,510	7,694,760	7,694,760

There are no gains or losses on translation into any reporting currency under the current method since the currency ledgers are technically balanced by spot exchange position accounts. On consolidation, these spot exchange position accounts are eliminated.

****

6. Open currency positions

Each FX trade is a position. If an investor buys a trade, he takes a long position. If he sells a trade, it is a short position. The open positions are in respect of relevant currency pairs. So long as the trade has not been closed out, his position is 'open'. Holding an open position is taking a risk, or betting, on exchange rate movements.

Banks look at 2 positions - the cash positions and the carry positions.

The cash positions:

Cash position in a currency is its net real assets and liabilities. This is the currency mismatch, which is the spot exchange position account balance. A credit balance in this account means the bank has more assets than liabilities in the relevant currency, i.e. it has a long position in that currency. A debit balance means it has more liabilities than assets, i.e. a short position in that currency.

Some call this the cash position, some call it the spot exchange position, others go by more fanciful terms. It's just terminology. Just remember that if it is called cash position, it does not pertain to cash as money in the banks. Instead, it refers to cash as on-balance sheet assets less liabilities. On the other hand, if referred to as spot exchange position, it is not about the trading spot position of FX traders which refers to currency pairs due for delivery in 2 days time.

The author recalls almost all visiting external auditors believed the cash position is the cash balances in the nostro accounts. This is a common error.

The carry positions:

This is an inventory of FX contracts that has not yet reached maturity dates. At any one time, banks hold, or carry, hundreds if not thousands, of FX contracts still outstanding. These contracts form the banks' open forward exchange positions. These are off balance sheet accounts.

Open positions in the forward market are comprised of all FX contracts outstanding. Trades are done in currency pairs, and forward exposures are viewed in terms of currency pairs. If all the deals in a particular pair of currencies, e.g USD/SGD, were aggregated, the net mismatch may be determined.

Fig.7 List of outstanding USD/SGD FX deals

				USD		SGD	
Ref	Deal date	Value date	Rate	Bought	Sold	Bought	Sold
1235467	1 Oct 2021	1 Nov 2021	1.3560	2,000,000			2,712,000
1234568	1 Oct 2021	3 Oct 2021	1.3500	4,000,000			5,400,000
1234569	3 Oct 2021	3 Oct 2021	1.3505		1,500,000	2,025,750	
1234570	4 Oct 2021	3 Jan 2021	1.3800	1,500,000			2,070,000
1234571	4 Oct 2021	3 Mar 2021	1.3900		2,000,000	2,780,000	
1234572	5 Oct 2021	4 Oct 2022	1.3560		1,000,000	1,356,000	
				7,500,000	4,500,000	6,161,750	10,182,000

Fig. 7 shows for USD/SGD, the bank has USD7.5m purchased and USD4.5m sold so there is a net purchase of USD3m. The bank has a long position of USD3m in USD/SGD pair. In the accounts, the USD ledger will show a credit balance of USD3m in the Forward exchange position account USD/SGD. The SGD ledger will show a debit balance of SGD4,020,250 in the Forward exchange position account USD/SGD.

Thus at any time a bank may be long in USD/SGD, short in USB/JPY, long in USD/EUR, short in USB/AUD etc.

FX maturity ladder:

The FX desk would be looking at open positions in a spectrum of maturity ladders, notably spot (which includes 1 day), 7 days, 1 month, 2 month, 3 month 6 month 12 month and beyond. They would look at individual currency pairs.

Mark-to-market:

Banks watch their risks to capital from exchange rate fluctuations by daily computation of fair values on their foreign exchange portfolio and spot exchange positions.

Chapter 12 shows how open forward positions are revalued and chapter 14 shows how open spot exchange positions are revalued.

****

7. Foreign exchange basics

This is not a primer on foreign exchange trading. Only the basics are mentioned to help understand accounting aspects.

Base currency / Quote currency:

In an exchange rate, 1 unit of currency X is equal to so many units of currency Y. Currency X is the base currency and Y is the quote currency. Eg USD/SGD rate is 1.3500. USD is the base currency and SGD is the quote currency. The base currency is the denominator, i.e., the currency which remains fixed whilst the other currency which is variable is the quote currency.

Currency pairs:

To state the obvious, FX is traded in pairs of currencies. An example is USD/SGD. The first currency is always the base currency. So a rate like SGD/MNT 2,2307.19 means 1 SGD = 2,307.19 Mongolian Tughrik.

Who determines which currency is the base currency of a currency pair. This is simply a matter of market convention. For currencies paired with USD, the base currency is usually USD due to its dominance. There are some exceptions, like GBP/USD and EUR/USD.

Cross rates:

Certain currencies are not quoted in certain places. Both currencies will then be referred to a third currency to derive a rate for the pair. These are known as cross rates. Eg there is no direct quote between Singapore dollars and Mongolian Tughrik. If USD/SGD rate is 1.3900 and USD/MNT is 3,207.00 then SGD/MNT is computed as 2,307.19.

In market practice, any currency pair that does not include USD is called a cross rate. The major cross rates include EUR/GBP, EUR/JPY, EUR/CHF, AUD/CHF.

Reciprocal / Non-reciprocal quotes:

A non-reciprocal quote for a currency pair is one where the base currency is the denominator. Eg USD/SGD 1.3580 i.e., 1 USD = 1.3580 SGD. USD is the denominator, thus 1.3580/1 = 1.3580.

A reciprocal quote for a currency pair is one where the base currency is the numerator. Thus the reciprocal rate of USD/SGD 1.3580 is 1/1.3580 = 0.7364, i.e., 1 SGD = o.7364 USD.

Direct/indirect quotes:

We talk about direct/indirect quotes in domestic situations. A direct quote for a currency pair is one where the rate is expressed in units of foreign currency to one unit of domestic currency. An indirect quote for a currency pair is one where the rate is expressed in domestic currency to one unit of foreign currency. Thus to Americans, USD/SGD of 1.3580 is a direct quote, for Singaporeans, that is an indirect quote.

Forward exchange deal:

This is a contract to exchange agreed amounts of currencies at an agreed rate at a predetermined date in the future.

Exchange-traded market (Spot FX market):

Currency trading is conducted through brokers whose FX trading platforms allow 24x7 online trading. Different terms and conditions apply depending on the exchange, such as margins, currencies traded, lot sizes, etc. The exchange displays quotes from participants. This is a spot market and there is no delivery. Trades are closed out before a certain time. Traders can roll over the trade if they do not wish to close out, subject to a fee.

OTC Market (Forward FX market):

OTC (Over The Counter) is a network of dealers. This is a market for FX rates for value dates of 3 days and beyond. Settlement is required and the counter-party delivery risk is high. This market deals mostly with the lesser traded and illiquid currencies in varying lot sizes.

Interbank Market:

Banks trade in the interbank market. In this case, banks trade directly with counter parties. There are no restrictions on lot sizes subject to a bank's trading limits for their counter parties. Trades are settled on value dates. The disadvantage of retail and business trading through banks is the price. As a middleman, banks add a profit margin or spread in their rates to customers.

Currency Futures Market:

Currency futures are forward-dated FX traded in an exchange such as CME. So lot sizes, non-delivery, margins and exchange rules apply. If a trade is not closed by the value date, delivery is required.

Lot size:

In the FX Exchanges, trades are conducted in standard lots of 100,000 units of base currency. Mini lot is 10,000, micro is 1,000. Interbank and OTC markets have no size restrictions other than the counter-party limits that traders maintain for each other.

Bid rate-offer rate:

Rates are quoted in two ways, a bid rate (buying) and an offer rate (selling). When a bank makes a quote, the bid rate is what he is willing to pay for the base currency. His offer rate is what he is willing to sell the base currency for. The 2-way quote is a tactic to hide whether the bank is interested in buying or selling. The bid rate is lower than the offer rate (buy low/sell high) and the difference is known as the spread. The spread is the cost of a trade.

Cash rate:

Cash rates are for immediate delivery. Examples are money changer rates, credit cards, bank teller transactions.

Tom rate:

Tom is short for tomorrow. This is a rate for delivery on the next business day. A deal on Monday is for delivery on Tuesday.

Spot rate:

The rate is for value over 2 business days. A deal struck on Monday is for delivery Wednesday.

Outright forward rate:

This is a rate for value 3 business days and beyond. Typically quoted in interbank for 7 days, 1 month, 3 months, 6 months, and 12 months. However, specific future dates are possible.

Tom-next:

This is a simultaneous buy/sell or sell/buy for Tom that takes place the next 2 days, eg deal done Monday buy value Tuesday and sell value Wednesday. This is used to roll over a trade when a trader does not want to close out a position (in the exchange market) or make delivery (in the OTC or interbank market).

FX swaps:

FX swaps are simultaneous buy/sell or sell/buy. Tom-next is a 1 day swap. FX swaps can cover longer periods. Whilst Tom-next is for rolling over a deal, swaps are for hedging over a longer time horizon.

Swap points:

The difference between the spot buy/sell and the forward sell/buy rates in a swap is known as swap points or forward pips. The swap points are calculated primarily from interest differentials between the 2 currencies.

Book rate:

This is the rate the accounts department uses for currency revaluation and translation for financial reporting purposes. There is no standard way. Middle offices of banks typically average the mid-points of a few reference banks' bid-offer rates.

Pips:

A pip is simply a measurement of a change in value between two currencies. It is represented by the last decimal value in a rate. Exchange rates are normally up to 4 decimal places (but some, like the JPY, have 2 decimal places). So the market is mostly on 4-2 decimal place system. Sometimes an additional point is added, and that is called a pipette.

E.g USD/SGD 1.3547

- 1.35470 = 13,547 pips
- 3 = 3,547 pips
- 5 = 547 pips
- 4 = 47 pips
- 7 = 7 pips
- 0 = nil pipettes

****

8. How to compute FX gains or losses

A pip is the smallest value change in an exchange rate. FX traders watch pip movements to monitor their profitability. Foreign exchange trading for private traders is highly leveraged. In the case of banks, their volumes are massive and lot sizes are in tens of millions. For both, every single pip movement may change the value of their trades significantly.

Illustration:

Bought 100,000 USD/SGD at 1.3560. Closed out at 1.3580 In a trading quote, the number of units refer to the base currency. Hence the 100,000 units in the example here refers to USD.

- <u>Check change in pips</u>
  Deal rate less close out rate.
  1.3560-1.3580 = 20 pips (an increase)
  In a purchase of a base currency, an increase in pips means a profit (See Fig.8 pip movement profitability matrix below).

- <u>Calculate the value per pip in the quote currency</u>
  Multiply the number of base currency units by 0.0001.
  100,000 units x 0.0001 = 10.
  This means for every 1 pip change in the rate the gain or loss is SGD10.
  Explanation:
  The base currency is the fixed currency. The impact of rate change is on the quote currency which is the variable.
  Deal rate for every 1 USD unit @ 1.3560 = SGD1.3560
  Thus 100,000 USD units @ 1.3560 = SGD135,600
  Thus 100,000 USD units @ 1.3561 = SGD135,610 = a P&L of SGD10 for an increase of 1 pip.

1. <u>Calculate value per pip value in the base currency</u>
   Take the per pip value in quote currency divided by close-out rate.
   10/1.3580=7.36
   For every 1 pip change in the rate, the gain or loss is USD7.36

- <u>To compute P&L in terms of quote currency</u>
  Calculate the change in pips x value per pip in the quote currency

20 x SGD10 = SGD200.00

- <u>To compute P&L in base currency</u>
  Calculate the change in pips x value per pip in the base currency
  20 x USD7.36 = USD147.20

The math can be proven by simple logic:

- If the trader bought USD100,000, at 1.3560 he paid SGD135,600. At 1.3580 the USD100,000 received is now worth SGD135,800. Thus a profit of SGD200.
- He paid SGD135,600 at 1.3560 and received USD100,000. The SGD135,600 now can be exchange for only USD99,853 at 1.3580, thus a profit of USD147.

How to know if it is a profit or loss:

Whether a movement in a pip means a profit or loss depends on :

- whether it is a long or short position, AND
- whether it is an increase or decrease in rates.

This pips profitability matrix is a good guide:

Fig.8 PIP Profitability Matrix

	Movement in PIPs	
	Increase	Decrease
Long position (buy)	PROFIT	LOSS
Short position (sell)	LOSS	PROFIT

In an FX trade, a buy is a long position. When a trader buys a currency pair, he is betting that one currency will appreciate against the other currency. So which currency is he favoring? In a buy, the trader holds the base currency, i.e., the first currency in the quoted pair. E.g. when he buys 100,000 EUR/USD he holds EUR, betting it will appreciate against the USD, i.e. he is long in EUR/USD position

A short position is the opposite. If he executes a sell EUR/USD order, he takes a negative position on EUR against USD.

In a forward FX (with delivery), the contract is buy USD100,000, sell SGD 135,600. We say the bank is long in USD/SGD. On delivery, the contract creates for the bank a long position in the buy currency and short in the sell currency.

Since the profit or loss can be in terms of either currency in a trading pair, which currency should it be based on? For a trader on an FX Exchange, the currency in which the profit or loss will be settled depends on the trading platform's administrative policy. Most use USD mainly because margin deposits are also in USD. Banks need an accounting policy to be established on which currency to book the profit or loss.

****

9. How to compute forward exchange rates

The previous chapter showed how FX gains or losses can be computed. It relied on a comparison of the contracted rate to a rate that has moved. In the case of realised exchange gains or losses, this is the spot rate at the time the contract was closed out or delivered. For unrealised exchange gains or losses, it is the expected forward rate that is being compared to. This chapter shows how the expected forward rate can be computed.

Interest Rate Parity:

Spot exchange rates are driven by market forces of supply and demand, which in turn is driven by liquidity. Forward exchange rates are influenced by the Interest Rate Parity principle.

IRP is a very significant theory in international finance that best explains how future exchange rate values are determined. It also explains why they fluctuate as they do. This is the basis used to compute the expected forward rate to compare to the contracted forward rates. It is the basis for revaluation of forward FX gains or losses.

The IRP theory describes the relationship between the spot exchange rate and the forward exchange rate of the two currencies involved, based on interest rates. To put it another way, the difference in the interest rates of the two currencies helps set forward rates. If there is currency equilibrium, the forward rates thus derived is the expected future spot rate. Currency equilibrium is a state where everything remains unchanged, i.e., the dynamics of supply of currency is constan.

The formula for IRP:

The forward exchange rate should be equal to the spot currency exchange rate times the interest rate of the quote currency, divided by the interest rate of the base currency.

$$FER = \frac{SER \times (1+q \times T)}{(1+b \times T)}$$

FER = Forward exchange ra

SER = Spot exchange rate

b = Interest rate of base currency

q = Interest rate of quote currency

T = Time or days left to maturity

Note: If base or quote is confusing, always remember the first currency in the currency pair is the base. Alternatively, you can remember the base currency as the denominator, i.e. the currency with 1 unit in the rate (1 unit of the base currency = x units of the quote currency).

Calculating the forward rate:

Current date : 11 Mar 2022
Date of contract: 10 Oct 2021
Value Date :10 Mar 2023 (ie days to maturity from current date is 1 year)
Deal rate : 1.1570
Purchased : USD1,000,000
Sold : EUR864,304
Spot rate for EUR/USD on current date : 1.0914
USD interest rate : 2%
EUR interest rate : 3%

$$FER = \frac{1.0914 \times (1+0.02) \times 365/365}{(1+0.03) \times 365/365}$$

$$=1.0808$$

Proofing the IRP:

When looking at a foreign currency with higher interest rate, an investor may think it is better to invest in that rather than in the home currency. Let's suppose an investor is considering placing his money in a 1 year fixed term deposit. He can place it in his home currency which earns a lower interest, or he can convert to the foreign currency to earn a higher interest. He can also convert the principal plus interest back to home currency on maturity. The underlying concept behind IRP is that, given currency equilibrium conditions, it doesn't make any difference which currency to invest. Because interest rates and forward currency rates are intertwined, the investor makes the same amount of money either way. In other words, no arbitrage opportunity exists.

Suppose on 11 Mar 2022 an investor has USD1,000,000 to invest. Since EUR earns a higher interest, he thinks he is better off investing in EUR. So he converts the USD to EUR at current spot rate, invest the EUR in a year term fixed deposit, and on maturity converts back to USD. Using the data in the above calculation the math is as follows:

- On 11 Mar 2022 convert USD to EUR using current spot rate:
  USD1,000,000/1.0914 = EUR916,254

- Principal + interest on maturity =
  EUR principal + interest @ 3% for 1 year:
  EUR916,254 x 1.03 x 1 year = EUR943,742

- On 10 Mar 2023 convert back to USD:
  EUR943,542 x 1.0808 = USD1,019,994

- Had he invested in USD, the principal + interest of 2% p.a. after 1 year would be:
  USD1,000,000 x 1.02 = USD1,020,000

Leaving the forward position open, he hopes to convert EUR P+I of EUR943,542 back to USD on maturity thus profiting from higher interest earned. But what would the rate be come 10 Mar 2023? Based on IRP, the forward rate computed at start date is 1.080. This is the expected spot rate for 10 Mar 2023 computed on 11 Mar 2022. With currency equilibrium, this forward rate converges with the spot rate at the end date. If IRP runs true, the investor finds he will convert back to about USD1,020,000. The returns to investor is exactly the same as had he invested in USD. This is known as an 'uncovered IRP'.

Suppose the investor does not want to take the open forward risk. On 11 Mar 2022, he asks the bank for a forward contract value 10 Mar 2023 to cover the EUR principal + interest to USD. This is known as a 'covered IRP'. In this case, the bank will compute a forward rate which will be 1.0808 (plus a small spread). This makes no difference to investor.

The question is, will the spot rate on maturity (10 Mar 2023) be 1.0808 as computed on start date (11 Mar 2022)? IRP theory rests on there being currency equilibrium, meaning currency supply and demand dynamics remain unchanged. If there is currency equilibrium, the forward rate calculated on 11 Mar 2022 is the expected rate. It will be the spot rate of the future date. To put it another way, the expected rate of a future date computed today will converge with the spot rate of the future date. Thus whether covered or uncovered, there is no arbitrage opportunity.

If there is currency equilibrium, it is possible to compute forward rates for 7 days, 1 month, 3 month, 6 months, 1 year, etc. This can be plotted in a chart known as the FX forward curve

Fig.9 The expected forward rate (FX forward curve)

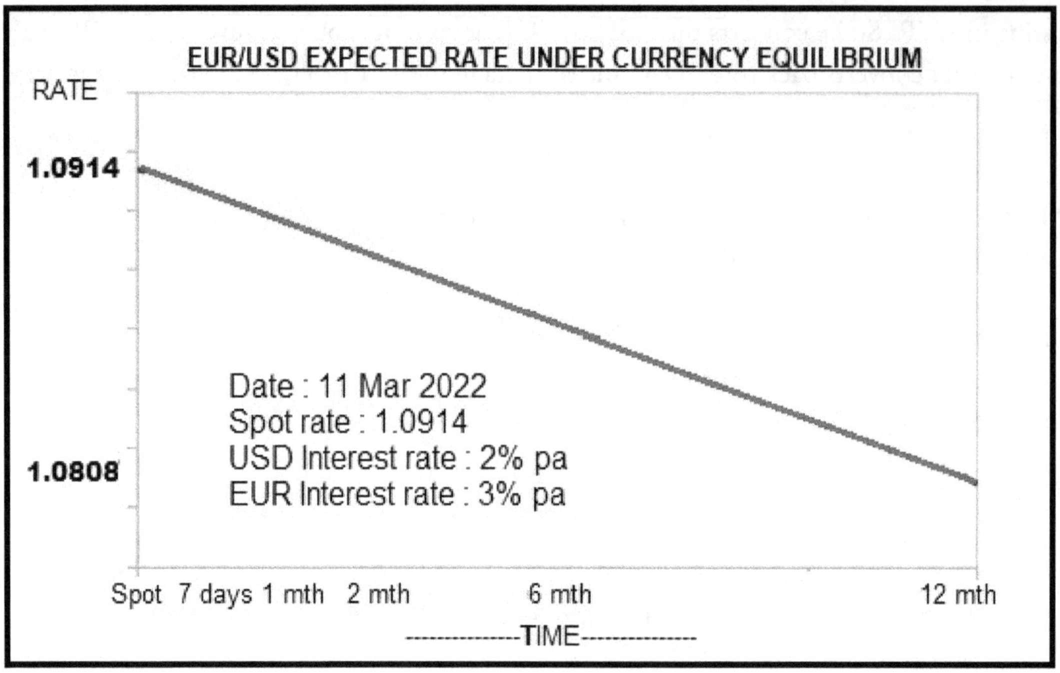

Currency equilibrium can be disrupted by many economic dynamics such as changes in trade patterns, tweaking of monetary policies of central banks, war, natural disasters that impact commodity supply and demand, etc. Thus the further the horizon, the higher the risk that IRP may not hold.

While traders consider risk factors, the accounting office simply works on the basis of IRP validity.

<u>Computing the profit & loss:</u>

With the expected forward rate, FX contracts can be revalued, or marked-to-market. Using the example above, the P&L can be calculated by following the steps in the previous chapter.

- Pip value in quote currency terms :
  Take units of base currency x 0.0001 (864,304 x 0.0001) = 86.43 USD
- Pip value in base currency terms :
  Take quote currency pip value divided by revaluation: (86.43/1.0808) = 79.97 EUR
- Pip movement is deal rate less revaluation rate:
  (1.1570-1.0808) = 762 (a decrease)

Since this is a sale of the base currency, a decrease in pips means a profit.
In USD terms : 762 x 86.43 USD = USD65,860 profit
In EUR terms : 762 x 79.97 EUR = EUR60,937 profit
(USD65,860 = EUR60,937 @ 1.0808)

Proof:

- Trader bought USD1,000,000, at 1.1570, he paid EUR 864,304. At 1.0808 the USD1,000,000 received is now worth EUR925,241. Thus a profit of EUR60,937.
- He paid EUR864,304 at 1.1570 and received USD1,000,000. The EUR864,304 can now be exchanged for only USD934,140 1.10808, thus a profit of USD65,860

****

10. Book rate maintenance

Terminologies may be confusing. So far we have covered :

- Base currency : This is the first currency in a currency pair. Eg in USD/SGD pair, USD is the base currency. This means where a quote is shown eg USD/SGD 1.3500, it means 1 USD = 1.35 SGD. (The other currency is the 'Quote' currency)
- Home currency : This is the local currency of the accounting entity and primarily used as the bookkeeping currency.
- Foreign currencies : These are the currencies of other countries outside of the accounting entities' home country.
- Functional currency : This is the currency which is not the home currency and which the entities use for bookkeeping because the bulk of their economic activities are in this currency.
- Book currency which is the recording unit used in the bookkeeping (could be any of the 4 mentioned above).

In multi-currency systems, a set of ledgers is opened for each currency which the entity has business activities in. Banks operate with numerous currency ledgers. As far as the accounting goes, there is no such thing as foreign currencies. However the system still requires a currency to be set as the core currency for all the other currencies to relate to so that currency-consolidated financial reports can be generated. This is the currency that has a value of '1' in relation to all the other currencies.

For our purpose, we call this core currency the book base currency and the others 'other currencies'. The book base currency could be any of the currencies. Logically it would be the currency in which the bank has most economic activities in. The rates input to the system are units of each 'other currency' in relation to "1" unit of the book base currency.

The system book rates are maintained before the close of business each day. For consistency, it is done at a specific time. The Accounting office performs the task independently of the Treasury Department or FX desk.

The Accounting office receives indicative quotes from 3 or 4 Reference banks. The bid-offer spot rates are obtained for various currency pairs the banks have business in.

In addition to exchange rates, the Accounting office also receives reference interbank money market rates. Rates are across several maturity bands—overnight, 7 days, months 1,3,6,12. These are rates without spreads. Reference benchmark is currently in a flux as the industry is going through reforms to replace LIBOR, SIBOR, HKBOR etc, which are money market rates offered daily by certain reference banks in the relevant market. The financial industry is moving away from reference bank quotes following the scandals of rate-fixing, to some form of actual transaction-based quotes.

Each currency is paired with the book base currency and forward premiums or discounts are calculated for each time band. The forward rate deduct the spot rate expressed in pips are known as swap points. When the swap points are positive, the base currency is at a premium to the quote currency. It is at a discount if the swap points are negative. The reference spot rates, premiums or discounts for each 'other' currency are then input to the system. The end-of-day system run has the capability to pro-rate the rates within the time bands to the number of days to maturity for each deal. This is how most accounting systems in banks work.

The book base rate for FX is thus the mid-point of average market spot rates for the day.

****

11. Foreign exchange deal life cycle

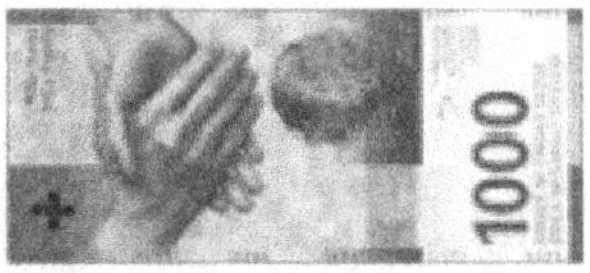

Suppose a bank has assets and liabilities like this :

Fig.10 Assets-Liabilities before FX deals

	Ledger: USD		Ledger: SGD		Ledger: AUD	
	Assets	Liabilities	Assets	Liabilities	Assets	Liabilities
Other assets-liabilities	5,000,000	5,000,000	325,000	325,000	219,150	219,150
Nostro	0	0	0	0	0	0
Spot exchange position	0	0	0	0	0	0
TOTAL	5,000,000	5,000,000	325,000	325,000	219,150	219,150
Off-Balance Sheet:						
FX purchased	0	0	0	0	0	0
FX sold	0	0	0	0	0	0
Fwd exc position USD/SGD	0	0	0	0	0	0
Fwd exc position USD/AUD	0	0	0	0	0	0
TOTAL	0	0	0	0	0	0

Bank writes 2 FX contracts :

- FX deal #1 buy 100,000 USD/SGD at 1.3500 value 7 days.
- FX deal #2 buy 55,000 USD/AUD at 1.4700 value 3 months.

Deal inception - Entries for FX deal #1 :

VR11-1	Ccy	Dr	Cr
USD LEDGER : Accounts			
FX purchased	USD	100,000	
Forward exc position USD/SGD	USD		100,000
SGD LEDGER : Accounts			
Forward exc position USD/SGD	SGD	135,000	
FX sold	SGD		135,000

Deal inception - Entries for FX deal #2 :

VR11-2	Ccy	Dr	Cr
USD LEDGER : Accounts			
FX purchased	USD	55,000	
Forward exc position USD/AUD	USD		55,000
AUD LEDGER : Accounts			
Forward exc position USD/AUD	AUD	80,850	
FX sold	AUD		80,850

Note:

1. The forward exchange contracts are record in the forward book. The accounts are all contingent items and do not appear in the real Asset & Liability Statements.
2. FX Purchased and FX Sold are control account entries with aggregated amounts posted. For clarity of illustration purpose here, individual FX deal entries are shown. Details are in the subsidiary ledger where transactions with counter-parties or customers are recorded. Subsidiary ledger is critical for managing counterparty risks.
3. The result of a forward FX deal is an imbalance in both currency ledgers in the forward book.
4. The Forward Exchange Position a/c is used to balance the mismatch in the forward currency ledgers.
5. Forward exposures are viewed in terms of currency pairs.

Fig.11 Assets-Liabilities after FX deal inception

	Ledger: USD		Ledger: SGD		Ledger: AUD	
	Assets	Liabilities	Assets	Liabilities	Assets	Liabilities
Other assets-liabilities	5,000,000	5,000,000	325,000	325,000	219,150	219,150
Nostro	0	0	0	0	0	0
Spot exchange position	0	0	0	0	0	0
TOTAL	5,000,000	5,000,000	325,000	325,000	219,150	219,150
Off-Balance Sheet:						
FX purchased	155,000	0	0	0	0	0
FX sold	0	0	0	135,000	0	80,850
Fwd exc position USD/SGD		100,000	135,000	0	0	0
Fwd exc position USD/AUD	0	55,000	0	0	80,850	0
TOTAL	155,000	155,000	135,000	135,000	80,850	80,850

Suppose FX deal #1 now matures and is settled. The bank receives USD100,000 and pays out SGD135,000.

Entries for deal settlement of FX Deal #1

VR11-3	Ccy	Dr	Cr
USD LEDGER : Accounts			
Forward exc position USD/SGD	USD	100,000	
FX purchased	USD		100,000
Nostro	USD	100,000	
Spot exchange position	USD		100,000
SGD LEDGER : Accounts			
FX sold	SGD	135,000	
Forward exc position USD/SGD	SGD		135,000
Spot exchange position	SGD	135,000	
Nostro	SGD		135,000

Note:

1. On value date, the forward positions are reversed into cash positions. The currencies move from contingent or forward book, to the cash book of real assets and liabilities.
2. Settlement is via Nostro accounts. These are the bank's operating accounts maintained with their correspondents. Eg the Singapore bank may maintain a USD a/c with Citibank (NY) to receive or pay USD, and Commonwealth Bank of Australia, Sydney, to pay and receive AUD, etc. Settlement of domestic currency is via banks' reserve accounts with the Central Bank. Eg Singapore banks settle SGD through reserve accounts with the MAS.
3. The result of a settled deal is a cash asset-liability mismatch in both currencies. The 'Spot Exchange Position A/c' is used to balance the mismatch in the ledgers of the two currencies.

Fig. 12 Assets-Liabilities after settlement of FX Deal #1

	Ledger: USD		**Ledger: SGD**		**Ledger: AUD**	
	Assets	Liabilities	Assets	Liabilities	Assets	Liabilities
Other assets-liabilities	5,000,000	5,000,000	325,000	325,000	219,150	219,150
Nostro	100,000	0	0	135,000		
Spot exchange position	0	100,000	135,000	0	0	0
TOTAL	5,100,000	5,100,000	460,000	460,000	219,150	219,150
Off-Balance Sheet:						
FX purchased	55,000	0	0	0	0	0
FX sold	0	0	0	0	0	80,850
Fwd exc position USD/SGD	0	0	0	0	0	0
Fwd exc position USD/AUD	0	55,000	0	0	80,850	0
TOTAL	55,000	55,000	0	0	80,850	80,850

Transactions involving exchange of 2 currencies create assets-liabilities mismatches in the currency ledgers. The debit/credit mismatches are balanced off by the use of exchange position accounts, one for the spot or cash book in each currency ledger, and as many for the forward books as there are currency pairs traded. A credit balance in the position accounts means there is more assets than liabilities in that currency, i.e., a long position. A debit balance means a short position, more liabilities than assets.

When an FX deal is settled, it extinguishes the forward positions and the cashflow creates spot positions for the 2 currencies involved.

****

12. Unrealised forward exchange gains or losses

Accounting standards require banks to mark-to-market, i.e., revalue the outstanding forward exchange contracts. Computerised systems now permit daily revaluation. This is a very important part of a bank's daily accounting routine because of the huge inventory it carries and spot rate volatility. The foreign exchange desk monitors their own performance and computes their own P&L. The middle office manages its own valuation application. The two figures are compared daily. Should the ball park figures differ substantially, investigations follow.

The accounting entries for mark-to-market of outstanding foreign exchange trades :

(A) In a legacy single currency accounting system

In each accounting period, the monetary assets are marked-to-market. If the valuation is lower than book value, the asset depreciation is provided for and taken to profit and loss.

Illustration :

In period 1, securities were valued at less than book value by USD100,000.

VR12-1	Ccy	Dr	Cr
Accounts	Ccy	Dr	Cr
Loss on valuation	USD	100,000	
Provision for valuation losses	USD		100,000

In period 2, securities were valued at less than cost by USD80,000. Thus there was excess provision of USD20,000 brought forward from period 1 now no longer required.

VR12-2	Ccy	Dr	Cr
Accounts			
Provision for valuation losses	USD	20,000	
Gains in valuation	USD		20,000

(B) In a multi-currency accounting system:

Foreign exchange transactions in banks are distinguished by:

1. FX is a major part of their business
2. Their FX portfolio is huge
3. Exchange rates are volatile, and
4. Employment of technology.

For these reasons, forward FX trades are marked-to-market daily. Technology makes this task effortless.

For forward exchange revaluation in banks, the traditional accounting entries described in (A) above are inefficient as daily activities. The traditional method computes the incremental difference over an accounting period. For banks that perform daily revaluation, computing incrementally is inefficient. Computerised systems solve the problem by using a 'shadow-posting' mechanism. This basically describes a way of passing gross provisional entries and reversing them the next day, rather than computing daily incremental differences.

Revaluation of forward exchange positions is done by taking all outstanding FX trades to compare the contract rates to the expected rates. As described in chapter 9, the expected exchange rate is the rate at maturity computed on the interest rate parity principle. Banks have thousands of outstanding trades in their forward books. Fortunately, this computation is not a problem for a computerised system.

There are 2 things to note. First, a gain or loss in an FX trade can be viewed from the perspective of either currency in a traded pair. Banks need to determine which view to take and which currency to book gains or losses. Secondly, a revaluation will compute a difference. Whether that is a gain or a loss depends on (a) whether it is a long position (bought) or a short position (sell) and (b) whether the rate has gone up or down. Refer to Fig.8 in chap 8 for 'pip profitability matrix'.

Illustration:

FX Deal #3 : Bank bought 100,000 USD/SGD at 1.1000 on May 25, value June 2.
Assume the bank books the exchange gains or losses in USD. The bank closes accounts monthly.

On May 25 the valuation and entries are:

Val12-1	Ccy	Amount	Rate	Ccy	Amount
FX Deal #3					
Contract	SGD	110,000	1.1000	USD	100,000
Expected rate Jun 2	SGD	110,000	1.2800	USD	85,938
Gains				USD	14,062

(Purchase base currency and an increase in rate = gains in exchange)

VR12-3	Ccy	Dr	Cr
USD LEDGER : Accounts			
Forward exc revaluation	USD	14,062	
Unrealised exchange p&l	USD		14,062

The expected rate changes each day due to (a) decreasing number of days to maturity and its impact on the interest differentials between the 2 currencies, and (2) changes in the spot rate. Day to day changes in the expected rate is very minimal unless there has been a big movement in the spot rate. For our purpose here, the expected rates are exaggerated for impact.

Suppose the forward revaluation for deal #3 goes like this :

Tab12-1			
Date	Ccy	Amount	
May 25	USD	14,062	gains
May 26	USD	12,200	gains
May 27	USD	11,220	gains
May 28	USD	3,240	gains
May 29	USD	-5,000	loss
May 30	USD	-3,100	loss
May 31	USD	1,150	gains
Jun 1	USD	4,200	gains

Each day, the previous day's entries will be reversed and new revaluation figures posted. The Unrealised Exchange P&L a/c will look like this.

AC12-2	Account : Unrealised Exchange p&l			
Date	Details	Dr	Cr	Balance
		USD	USD	USD
May 25	Forward revaluation gains		14,062	14,062
May 26	Forward revaluation reversal	-14,062		0
May 26	Forward revaluation gains		12,200	12,200
May 27	Forward revaluation reversal	-12,200		0
May 27	Forward revaluation gains		11,220	11,220
May 28	Forward revaluation reversal	-11,220		0
May 28	Forward revaluation gains		3,240	3,240
May 29	Forward revaluation reversal	-3,240		0
May 29	Forward revaluation loss	-5,000		-5,000
May 30	Forward revaluation reversal		5,000	0
May 30	Forward revaluation loss	-3,100		-3,100
May 31	Forward revaluation reversal		3,100	0
May 31	Forward revaluation gains		1,150	1,150
May 31	Transfer to Profit & Loss	-1,150		0
Jun 1	Forward revaluation reversal	-1,150		-1,150
Jun 1	Forward revaluation gains		4,200	3,050
Jun 2	Forward revaluation reversal	-4,200		-1,150

The revaluation gains/losses are posted to the revenue account (Unrealised Exchange p&l) at the end-of-day run. The entry is reversed at the next start-of-day run. So the unrealised Exchange P&L a/c starts with fresh slate each day. Losses are treated in a similar fashion, but on the different side of the T-account, shown here in red type to highlight.

Note what happens when crossing into the next accounting period. As the bank closes their accounts monthly, the end-of-month run transfers all revenue and expenses accounts to equity, the Profit & Loss Account. On the first day of the next accounting period, the forward revaluation gains of May 31 are reversed. This causes the revenue account to start the new accounting period June with a negative USD1,150. This means part of the gains of FX Deal #3 (USD1,150) has already been taken up in equity in May. This amount reduces the gains and losses figure for June.

Thus the revaluation for the deal on June 1 was USD4,200 but the revenue account shows only a net gain of USD3,050 because USD1,150 has been taken up in May.

When a forward FX deal matures on June 2, it is no longer in the portfolio. It simply disappears from the forward exchange revaluation. Thus reviewing the daily unrealised FX p&l may throw one off-track because wild swings are observed. This is not due to extreme rate changes but rather because of deals reaching maturity. As deals mature and get settled they leave the pool of outstanding trades that are being revalued. Thus causing big swings in the revaluation figures. A big swing in unrealised FX p&l is compensated by a reverse swing in realised FX p&l. An example explains this. Suppose a deal has been contributing a big unrealised gains of $40,000. On reaching maturity, it gets settled. Thus it leaves the pool of outstanding FX trades and $40,000 disappears from unrealised FX p&l. However, as it is settled, the deal contributes $40,000 to realised FX p&l.

What happens to matured deals is explained in the next chapter.

The entries here relate to a single trade, FX deal #3, for illustration purposes. The revaluation for the day is on the total forward FX portfolio. Aggregate gains or losses will be posted. Each day, new forward deals are added to the portfolio and matured deals are taken off automatically.

****

13. Realised exchange gains or losses

Continuing with FX deal #3.

FX Deal #3 : Bank bought 100,000 USD/SGD at 1.1000 on May 25, value June 2.

Assume the bank books the exchange gains or losses in USD. The bank closes accounts monthly. It is now June 2 and the deal has matured. There are 3 things to take care of.

1. Removal from the forward exchange position
2. Settlement or delivery of the trade ie, receipt and payment of currencies
3. Compute the realised exchange gains or losses.

(1) Removal from forward exchange position:

VR13-1	Ccy	Dr	Cr
USD LEDGER : Accounts			
Forward exc position USD/SGD	USD	100,000	
FX purchased	USD		100,000
SGD LEDGER : Accounts			
FX sold	SGD	110,000	
Forward exc position USD/SGD	SGD		110,000

(2) Settlement entries:

On value date, the FX trade is settled, which causes imbalances in the two currency ledgers. It creates a long (overbought) position in the USD, and a short (oversold) position in the SGD. Spot exchange position accounts are used as 'mirror' accounts to balance the ledgers.

VR13-2	Ccy	Dr	Cr
USD LEDGER : Accounts			
Nostro	USD	100,000	
Spot exchange position	USD		100,000
SGD LEDGER : Accounts			
Spot exchange position	SGD	110,000	
Nostro	SGD		110,000

(3) Realised exchange gains or losses and entries :

Val13-1	Ccy	Amount	Rate	Ccy	Amount
FX Deal #3					
Contract	SGD	110,000	1.1000	USD	100,000
Book rate Jun 2	SGD	110,000	1.1579	USD	95,000
Gains				USD	5,000

(Purchase base currency and an increase in rate = gains in exchange)

VR13-3	Ccy	Dr	Cr
USD LEDGER : Accounts			
Spot exchange position	USD	5,000	
Realised exchange p&l	USD		5,000

Note:

- Unrealised exchange gains or losses is the difference between contract rate and expected rate, whereas realised exchange gains or losses is between contract rate and book rate (which approximates market spot rates).
- Taking the realised exchange gains or losses in a currency creates a spot exchange position in that currency, in this case, the USD.

<u>How is this reflected in the Exchange P&L account:</u>

Continuing with the May statement from chapter 12, the exchange p&l accounts look like this.

AC13-1		Ac : Unrealised Exchange p&l	Dr	Cr	Balance
Date	Ref	Details	USD	USD	USD
Jun 1		B/f	0		0
Jun 1		Forward revaluation reversal	-1,150		-1,150
Jun 1		Forward revaluation gains		4,200	3,050
Jun 2		Forward revaluation reversal	-4,200		-1,150

AC13-2		Ac : Realised Exchange p&l	Dr	Cr	Balance
Date	Ref	Details	USD	USD	USD
Jun 2		Realised ex gains FX deal #3		5,000	5,000

The realised gains in June is USD5,000. The Unrealised Exchange P&L balance in the account is negative USD1,150 which is the forward gains already taken up in equity, or Profit & Loss A/c in May. Thus the overall exchange profit & loss for this FX deal #3 in June is only USD3,850 (5,000-1,150).

The above serves to illustrate one single deal for clarity. In practice, the system computes on a mass basis comprising of hundreds if not thousands of FX deals. It is not easy to read off operating reports, nevertheless, audit trails for individual FX deals are available for closer scrutiny if desired. Each day, new forward deals are added to the portfolio and matured deals are taken off the portfolio automatically. This illustration shows what happens to a single deal when it matures.

****

14. Spot exchange position revaluation

In banks' multi-currency systems, the settlement of an FX contract causes an assets-liabilities mismatch in the ledgers of the two currencies involved. Spot exchange position accounts are set up as mirror accounts in the ledgers of both currencies that allow the double-entry book-keeping to go through. As mirror or compensating accounts, they are eliminated when consolidated in a reporting currency.

Note the term 'spot' here does not refer to the 2-days delivery in FX trading. For our accounting purposes, it refers to a mismatch between cash or real assets and liabilities.

Spot exchange position account represents the relevant currency's real or cash net assets and liabilities. The value of these spot exchange position accounts in terms of the book base currency changes with daily market spot rates. Spot exchange position accounts have to be revalued in relation to the book base currency or else the currency ledgers cannot be reconciled in a presentation currency.

Illustration:

Assumption : The book base and reporting currency is USD. Gains or losses in foreign exchange are taken in the book base currency.

Suppose on Monday close-of-business the assets and liabilities look like this.

Fig.13 Monday Assets-Liabilities carried forward

	USD Ledger		SGD Ledger		AUD Ledger		Reporting USD	
	Assets	Liabilities	Assets	Liabilities	Assets	Liabilities	Assets	Liabilities
Other Assets-Liabilities	5,155,000	5,000,000	325,000	460,000	219,150	300,000	5,544,822	5,544,822
Nostro	0	0	0	0	0	0	0	0
Spot exchange position	0	155,000	135,000	0	80,850	0	155,000	155,000
Fwd Exc revaluation	0	0	0	0	0	0	0	0
Profit & Loss (equity)	0	0	0	0	0	0	0	0
Unrealised Exc p&l	0	0	0	0	0	0	0	0
Realised Exchange p&l	0	0	0	0	0	0	0	0
Spot exc revaluation p&l	0	0	0	0	0	0	0	0
TOTAL	5,155,000	5,155,000	460,000	460,000	300,000	300,000	5,699,822	5,699,822
Book rates	1.0000	1.0000	1.3500	1.3500	1.4700	1.4700		
Translated to USD	5,155,000	5,155,000	340,741	340,741	204,082	204,082	5,699,822	5,699,822

Notice the spot exchange position is eliminated when consolidated in a reporting currency.

Suppose on Tuesday there were no other transactions and the rate for SGD is now 1.3550, AUD is 1.4750.

Fig.14 Tuesday Assets-Liabilities BEFORE revaluation of spot exchange positions

	USD Ledger		SGD Ledger		AUD Ledger		Reporting USD	
	Assets	Liabilities	Assets	Liabilities	Assets	Liabilities	Assets	Liabilities
Other Assets-Liabilities	5,155,000	5,000,000	325,000	460,000	219,150	300,000	5,543,429	5,542,873
Nostro	0	0	0	0	0	0	0	0
Spot exchange position	0	155,000	135,000	0	80,850	0	154,445	155,000
Fwd Exc revaluation	0	0	0	0	0	0	0	0
Profit & Loss (equity)	0	0	0	0	0	0	0	0
Unrealised Exc p&l	0	0	0	0	0	0	0	0
Realised Exchange p&l	0	0	0	0	0	0	0	0
Spot exc revaluaton p&l	0	0	0	0	0	0	0	0
TOTAL	5,155,000	5,155,000	460,000	460,000	300,000	300,000	5,697,873	5,697,873
Book rates	1.0000	1.0000	1.3550	1.3550	1.4750	1.4750		
Translated to USD	5,155,000	5,155,000	339,483	339,483	203,390	203,390	5,697,873	5,697,873

The spot exchange positions do not cancel out. The reason being rates have changed. Spot position revaluation is now necessary. The figure to reconcile is **USD555** (155,000-155,445). On close of business Tuesday, the brought forward balance of spot exchange positions are revalued.

Revalue SGD spot exchange position b/f :

Val14-1	Ccy	Amount	Rate	Ccy	Amount
SGD spot exc position b/f					
Book rate Monday	SGD	135,000	1.35	USD	100,000
Book rate Tuesday	SGD	135,000	1.355	USD	99,631
Gains				USD	369

(Long position base currency and an increase in rate = gains in exchange)

In SGD books, the debit balance of SGD135,000 in spot exchange position means there was a net SGD cash liability. If we are revaluing against the book base currency ie USD, then the SGD (debit balance) is short against the USD. Thus USD is long and it is the base currency in USD/SGD, then an increase in the rate means a gain in exchange in USD terms.

Revalue AUD spot exchange position b/f :

Val14-2	Ccy	Amount	Rate	Ccy	Amount
AUD spot exc position b/f					
Book rate Monday	AUD	80,850	1.4700	USD	55,000
Book rate Tuesday	AUD	80,850	1.4750	USD	54,814
Gains				USD	186

(Long position base currency and an increase in rate = gains in exchange)

By the same reasoning as for the SGD, the AUD open spot exchange position saw a gain in exchange of USD186.

Spot exchange position revaluation entries :

VR14-1	Ccy	Dr	Cr
USD LEDGER : Accounts			
Spot exchange position	USD	555	
Exc revaluation p&l	USD		555

The total realised gains in exchange USD555 (369+186) is taken up in USD Ledger

Fig.14a Tuesday Assets-Liabilities AFTER revaluation of spot exchange positions

	USD Ledger		SGD Ledger		AUD Ledger		Reporting USD	
	Assets	Liabilities	Assets	Liabilities	Assets	Liabilities	Assets	Liabilities
Other Assets-Liabilities	5,155,000	5,000,000	325,000	460,000	219,150	300,000	5,543,429	5,542,873
Nostro	0	0	0	0	0	0	0	0
Spot exchange position	0	154,445	135,000	0	80,850	0	154,445	154,445
Fwd Exc revaluation	0	0	0	0	0	0	0	0
Profit & Loss (equity)	0	0	0	0	0	0	0	0
Unrealised Exc p&l	0	0	0	0	0	0	0	0
Realised Exchange p&l	0	0	0	0	0	0	0	0
Spot exc revaluaton p&l	0	555	0	0	0	0	0	555
TOTAL	5,155,000	5,155,000	460,000	460,000	300,000	300,000	5,697,873	5,697,873
Book rates	1.0000	1.0000	1.3550	1.3550	1.4750	1.4750		
Translated to USD	5,155,000	5,155,000	339,483	339,483	203,390	203,390	5,697,873	5,697,873

After revaluation of brought forward balances of spot exchange positions, the mirror accounts are eliminated on currency consolidation

No revaluation on spot exchange positions created in current day (Tuesday)

Let's back track to opening of business on Tuesday before spot exchange position revaluation. Suppose on Tuesday there was a same day value FX transaction.

FX deal #4 sold 50,000 USD/SGD at 1.3588 value Tuesday.

What the example FX deal #4 shows is new positions created by new transactions during current business day. This deal creates :

- Short position in USD of 50,000 (sold)
- Long position in SGD of 67,940 (bought)

Firstly we take care of deal inception entries:

VR14-2	Ccy	Dr	Cr
USD LEDGER : Accounts			
Forward exc position USD/SGD	USD	50,000	
FX sold	USD		50,000
SGD LEDGER : Accounts			
FX purchased	SGD	67,940	
Forward exc position USD/SGD	SGD		67,940

Secondly, the deal settlement entries:

VR14-3	Ccy	Dr	Cr
USD LEDGER : Accounts			
FX sold	USD	50,000	
Forward exc position USD/SGD	USD		50,000
Spot exchange position a/c	USD	50,000	
Nosro a/c	USD		50,000
SGD LEDGER : Accounts			
FX sold	SGD	76,940	
Forward exc position USD/SGD	SGD		67,940
Nosro a/c	SGD	76,940	
Spot exchange position a/c	SGD		76,940

Thirdly, we perform the realised exchange gains or losses on FX deal #4 and entries :

Val14-3	Ccy	Amount	Rate	Ccy	Amount
FX Deal #4					
Contract	SGD	67,940	1.3588	USD	50,000
Book rate Tuesday	SGD	67,940	1.3550	USD	50,141
Gains				USD	-141

(Sold base currency and a decrease in rate = gains in exchange)

VR14-4	Ccy	Dr	Cr
USD LEDGER : Accounts			
Spot exchange position	USD	141	
Realised exchange p&l	USD		141

The assets-liabilities will look like this:

Fig.14b Tuesday Assets-Liabilities BEFORE revaluation of spot exchange positions

	USD Ledger		SGD Ledger		AUD Ledger		Reporting USD	
	Assets	Liabilities	Assets	Liabilities	Assets	Liabilities	Assets	Liabilities
Other Assets-Liabilities	5,155,000	5,000,000	325,000	460,000	219,150	300,000	5,543,429	5,542,873
Nostro	0	50,000	67,940	0	0	0	50,140	50,000
Spot exchange position	0	104,859	67,060	0	80,850	0	104,304	104,859
Fwd Exc revaluation	0	0	0	0	0	0	0	0
Profit & Loss (equity)	0	0	0	0	0	0	0	0
Unrealised Exc p&l	0	0	0	0	0	0	0	0
Realised Exchange p&l	0	141	0	0	0	0	0	141
Spot exc revaluaton p&l	0	0	0	0	0	0	0	0
TOTAL	5,155,000	5,155,000	460,000	460,000	300,000	300,000	5,697,873	5,697,873
Book rates	1.0000	1.0000	1.3550	1.3550	1.4750	1.4750		
Translated to USD	5,155,000	5,155,000	339,483	339,483	203,390	203,390	5,697,873	5,697,873

Notice now when consolidated in USD, the spot exchange position accounts do not get eliminated. This is because we have not yet done the spot exchange position revaluation. Once again, the difference to reconcile is the same **USD555** (104,859-104,304 = 555) as in Table 14 above.

FX deal#4 has changed the spot exchange positions significantly, yet the amount to reconcile remains unchanged at USD555. What does this mean?

At the close of business each day, the spot exchange account balances comprise of:

- New positions created during the day.

Hundreds if not thousands of transactions, reached value date and get settled. -The resultant cashflows create new positions each day. FX deal #4 is just an example. These new positions are **excluded** from the daily revaluation computation on value date or day of settlement because they have already been revalued when accounting for realised exchange gains and losses.

- Brought forward positions from the previous day (Monday).

These positions were brought forward based on rates of the previous day. As exchange rates have changed these brought forward positions need to be revalued.

We are dealing with the same open positions as for Table 14a. Let's continue then.

Fourthly and finally, let's take care of the revaluation of brought forward spot exchange positions using the same computations and entries done for Table 14a above:

Revalue SGD spot exchange position b/f:

Val14-1	Ccy	Amount	Rate	Ccy	Amount
SGD spot exc position b/f					
Book rate Monday	SGD	135,000	1.35	USD	100,000
Book rate Tuesday	SGD	135,000	1.355	USD	99,631
Gains				USD	369

(Long position base currency and an increase in rate = gains in exchange)

Revalue AUD spot exchange position b/f:

Val14-2	Ccy	Amount	Rate	Ccy	Amount
AUD spot exc position b/f					
Book rate Monday	AUD	80,850	1.4700	USD	55,000
Book rate Tuesday	AUD	80,850	1.4750	USD	54,814
Gains				USD	186

(Long position base currency and an increase in rate = gains in exchange)

Spot exchange position revaluation entries :

VR14-1	Ccy	Dr	Cr
USD LEDGER : Accounts			
Spot exchange position	USD	555	
Exc revaluation p&l	USD		555

The assets-liabilities status on Tuesday close-of-business now looks like this:

Fig.15 Tuesday Assets-Liabilities AFTER revaluation of spot exchange positions

	USD Ledger		SGD Ledger		AUD Ledger		Reporting USD	
	Assets	Liabilities	Assets	Liabilities	Assets	Liabilities	Assets	Liabilities
Other Assets-Liabilities	5,155,000	5,000,000	325,000	460,000	219,150	300,000	5,543,429	5,542,873
Nostro	0	50,000	67,940	0	0	0	50,140	50,000
Spot exchange position	0	104,304	67,060	0	80,850	0	104,304	104,304
Fwd Exc revaluation	0	0	0	0	0	0	0	0
Profit & Loss (equity)	0	0	0	0	0	0	0	0
Unrealised Exc p&l	0	0	0	0	0	0	0	0
Realised Exchange p&l	0	141	0	0	0	0	0	141
Spot exc revaluaton p&l	0	555	0	0	0	0	0	555
TOTAL	5,155,000	5,155,000	460,000	460,000	300,000	300,000	5,697,873	5,697,873
Book rates	1.0000	1.0000	1.3550	1.3550	1.4750	1.4750		
Translated to USD	5,155,000	5,155,000	339,483	339,483	203,390	203,390	5,697,873	5,697,873

Note : The spot exchange position accounts can now be eliminated on consolidation in reporting currency.

The whole point of this illustration:

The purpose is to stress spot exchange position revaluation is done on brought forward balances in the accounts, not the close of business positions.

Spot exchange position revaluation in multi-currency accounting is in effect the legacy currency translation, but done on net currency assets-liabilities basis and performed daily by banks.

****

15. Daily accounting routine

Banks hold thousands of forward-dated FX deals in their portfolio and maintain open exchange positions within their risk parameters. In the context of foreign exchange gains or losses, banks perform daily the 3 main tasks of computing unrealised exchange p&l on forward FX deals, computing realised exchange p&l on FX deals that matured on the day, and revaluation of open spot exchange positions.

Daily accounting cycle:

1. Start-of-day run to reverse the unrealised exchange p&l entries of the previous day.
2. Enter new FX transactions
3. Post settlement entries of FX deals that matured during the day.
4. Before end-of-day, update book rates, currency discounts or premiums, and interest rates.
5. End-of day run to compute realised exchange gains/losses on FX deals that matured and post entries.
6. End-of-day run to compute unrealised exchange gains/losses on forward FX deals and post entries.
7. End-of-day run to compute revaluation on brought forward spot exchange positions, and post entries.
8. End-of-month run to close revenue/expense accounts to equity.

Apart from (4), all tasks would be automated by some banking system. The following illustrations walk through these tasks using a single FX deal at a time, and the effects monitored in the assets-liabilities status

Assumptions for following illustrations for month of May:

1. USD is the functional currency (which is also the system, or book base currency - the currency that has a value of 1 in relation to all the other currencies)
2. Reporting currency SGD
3. Exchange gains/losses are taken in USD whenever it is in a currency pair, <u>cross rates share gains/losses on a 50-50 basis.</u>
4. Revenue/expense accounts are closed to Profit & Loss a/c at month end.

****

15.1 May 1 : Starting off with no FX transactions

Assume commencement on May 1 with no currency mismatch.

Fig 16 Assets-Liabilities with no currency mismatch

1 May 2022	USD Ledger		SGD Ledger		AUD Ledger		Reporting SGD	
	Assets	Liabilities	Assets	Liabilities	Assets	Liabilities	Assets	Liabilities
Other Assets-Liabilities	5,000,000	5,000,000	3,000,000	3,000,000	200,000	200,000	9,184,615	9,184,615
Nostro	0	0	0	0	0	0	0	0
Spot exchange position	0	0	0	0	0	0	0	0
Fwd Exc revaluation	0	0	0	0	0	0	0	0
Profit & Loss (equity)	0	0	0	0	0	0	0	0
Unrealised Exc p&l	0	0	0	0	0	0	0	0
Realised Exchange p&l	0	0	0	0	0	0	0	0
Spot exc revaluaton p&l	0	0	0	0	0	0	0	0
TOTAL	5,000,000	5,000,000	3,000,000	3,000,000	200,000	200,000	9,184,615	9,184,615
Book rates	1.2000	1.2000	1.0000	1.0000	0.9231	0.9231		
Translated to SGD	6,000,000	6,000,000	3,000,000	3,000,000	184,615	184,615	9,184,615	9,184,615

****

15.2 May 2 : Forward FX deal & forward revaluation

Forward revaluation (mark-to-market of outstanding unmatured FX deals) are performed daily and posted.

Spot deal done : FX deal #5 - Bought 100,000 USD/SGD at 1.1000 Value May 4.

(1) Start-of-day run to reverse the unrealised exchange p&l entries of the previous day

Not applicable. No forward revaluation on May 1.

(2) Enter new FX transactions

Deal inception - FX deal #5

VR15-2-1	Ccy	Dr	Cr
USD LEDGER : Accounts			
FX purchased	USD	100,000	
Forward exc position USD/SGD	USD		100,000
SGD LEDGER : Accounts			
Forward exc position USD/SGD	SGD	110,000	
FX sold	SGD		110,000

(3) Post settlement entries of FX deals that matured during the day

Not applicable. No FX deals maturing.

(4) Update book-rates and currency discounts and premiums

USD/SGD : 1.2500; USD/AUD: 1.3500; AUD/SGD: 0.9259

(5) End-of day run to compute realised exchange gains/losses on FX deals that matured and post entries

Not applicable. No FX deals maturing.

(6) End-of-day run to compute unrealised exchange gains/losses on forward FX deals and post entries.

Forward revaluation is performed on inventory of outstanding FX deals. For illustration purpose, there is only a single FX deal #5.

Val15-2-1	Ccy	Amount	Rate	Ccy	Amount
FX Deal #5					
Contract	SGD	110,000	1.1000	USD	100,000
Expected rate May 4	SGD	110,000	1.2700	USD	86,614
Gains				USD	13,386

(Purchase base currency and an increase in rate = gains in exchange)

The 'expected rate' is discussed in the chapter 9. Assume it is 1.2700. Day-to-day changes are insignificant, unless there has been some ground shattering events in world affairs. For the purpose here, the expected rates are exaggerated to dramatise the effects.

VR15-2-2	Ccy	Dr	Cr
USD LEDGER : Accounts	Ccy	Dr	Cr
Forward exchange revaluation	USD	13,386	
Urealised Exchange p&l	USD		13,386

(7) **End-of-day run to compute revaluation on brought forward spot exchange positions, and post entries.**
Not applicable. There are no spot exchange positions brought forward

ASSETS & LIABILITIES AS AT MAY 2

Fig.17 Assets-Liabilities AFTER new forward FX deal and forward revaluation

2 May 2022	USD Ledger		SGD Ledger		AUD Ledger		Reporting SGD	
	Assets	Liabilities	Assets	Liabilities	Assets	Liabilities	Assets	Liabilities
Other Assets-Liabilities	5,000,000	5,000,000	3,000,000	3,000,000	200,000	200,000	9,435,185	9,435,185
Nostro	0	0	0	0	0	0	0	0
Spot exchange position	0	0	0	0	0	0	0	0
Fwd Exc revaluation	13,386	0	0	0	0	0	16,733	0
Profit & Loss (equity)	0	0	0	0	0	0	0	0
Unrealised Exc p&l	0	13,386	0	0	0	0	0	16,733
Realised Exchange p&l	0	0	0	0	0	0	0	0
Spot exc revaluaton p&l	0	0	0	0	0	0	0	0
TOTAL	5,013,386	5,013,386	3,000,000	3,000,000	200,000	200,000	9,451,918	9,451,918
Book rates	1.2500	1.2500	1.0000	1.0000	0.9259	0.9259		
Translated to SGD	6,266,733	6,266,733	3,000,000	3,000,000	185,185	185,185	9,451,918	9,451,918
OFF BALANCE SHEET:								
FX purchased	100,000	0	0	0	0	0		
FX sold	0	0	0	110,000	0	0		
Fwd exc position USD/SGD	0	100,000	110,000	0	0	0		
Fwd exc position USD/AUD	0	0	0	0	0	0		
Fwd exc position AUD/SGD	0	0	0	0	0	0		
	100,000	100,000	110,000	110,000	0	0		

Note : Forward exchange revaluation does not create any spot exchange positions. It is simply recorded in the book base currency in a revenue and suspense (or provision) account. There is a forward exchange position account for each currency pair.

****

15.3 May 3 : 'Shadow posting' effect of forward FX revaluation

The previous day's forward revaluation are reversed and current day's forward revaluation are computed and posted.

(1) Start-of-day run to reverse the forward revaluation entries of the previous day

VR15-3-1	Ccy	Dr	Cr
USD LEDGER : Accounts			
Unrealised exchange p&l	USD	13,386	
Forward exchange revaluation	USD		13,386

(2) Enter new FX transactions

Not applicable. No new transaction.

(3) Post settlement entries of FX deals that matured during the day

Not applicable. No FX deals maturing.

(4) Update book-rates and currency discounts and premiums

USD/SGD : 1.2800; USD/AUD: 1.3550; AUD/SGD: 0.9446

(5) End-of day run to compute realised exchange gains/losses on FX deals that matured and post entries

Not applicable. No FX deals maturing.

(6) End-of-day run to compute unrealised exchange gains/losses on forward FX deals and post entries.

There is only one single FX deal #5 outstanding.

Val15-3-1	Ccy	Amount	Rate	Ccy	Amount
FX Deal #5					
Contract	SGD	110,000	1.1000	USD	100,000
Expected rate May 4	SGD	110,000	1.2800	USD	85,938
Gains				USD	14,062

(Purchase base currency and an increase in rate = gains in exchange)

VR15-3-2	Ccy	Dr	Cr
USD LEDGER : Accounts			
Forward exchange revaluation	USD	14,062	
Unrealised Exchange p&l	USD		14,062

(7) End-of-day run to compute revaluation on brought forward spot exchange positions, and post entries.

Not applicable. There are no spot exchange positions in 'other currencies' brought forward.

ASSETS & LIABILITIES AS AT MAY 3

Fig 18 Assets-Liabilities and 'shadow posting' refresh of forward revaluation

3 May 2022	USD Ledger		SGD Ledger		AUD Ledger		Reporting SGD	
	Assets	Liabilities	Assets	Liabilities	Assets	Liabilities	Assets	Liabilities
Other Assets-Liabilities	5,000,000	5,000,000	3,000,000	3,000,000	200,000	200,000	9,588,930	9,588,930
Nostro	0	0	0	0	0	0	0	0
Spot exchange position	0	0	0	0	0	0	0	0
Fwd Exc revaluation	14,062	0	0	0	0	0	17,999	0
Profit & Loss (equity)	0	0	0	0	0	0	0	0
Unrealised Exc p&l	0	14,062	0	0	0	0	0	17,999
Realised Exchange p&l	0	0	0	0	0	0	0	0
Spot exc revaluaton p&l	0	0	0	0	0	0	0	0
TOTAL	5,014,062	5,014,062	3,000,000	3,000,000	200,000	200,000	9,606,929	9,606,929
Book rates	1.2800	1.2800	1.0000	1.0000	0.9446	0.9446		
Translated to SGD	6,417,999	6,417,999	3,000,000	3,000,000	188,930	188,930	9,606,929	9,606,929
OFF BALANCE SHEET:								
FX purchased	100,000	0	0	0	0	0		
FX sold	0	0	0	110,000	0	0		
Fwd exc position USD/SGD	0	100,000	110,000	0	0	0		
Fwd exc position USD/AUD	0	0	0	0	0	0		
Fwd exc position AUD/SGD	0	0	0	0	0	0		
	100,000	100,000	110,000	110,000	0	0		

****

15.4 May 4 : Settlement of FX deal

On maturity, the settlement of the matured FX deal creates a cashflow mismatch in the ledgers of the two currencies, ie it creates long or short positions in the 2 currencies.. This mismatch is balanced using spot exchange position accounts which are mirror accounts across the 2 books. Realised exchange gains or loss is recognised which also creates spot exchange positions.

(1) Start-of-day run to reverse the unrealised exchange p&l of the previous day

VR15-4-1	Ccy	Dr	Cr
USD LEDGER : Accounts			
Unrealised exchange p&l	USD	14,062	
Forward exchange revaluation	USD		14,062

(2) Enter new FX transactions

Not applicable. No new transaction.

(3) Post settlement entries of FX deals that matured during the day

FX#5 matured on May 4

VR15-4-2	Ccy	Dr	Cr
USD LEDGER : Accounts			
Forward exc position USD/SGD	USD	100,000	
FX purchased	USD		100,000
Nostro	USD	100,000	
Spot exchange position	USD		100,000
SGD LEDGER : Accounts			
FX sold	SGD	110,000	
Forward exc position USD/SGD	SGD		110,000
Spot exchange position	SGD	110,000	
Nostro	SGD		110,000

Note: On settlement, FX deals cause currency mismatch, or create open spot exchange positions, in the 2 currencies involved.

(4) Update book-rates and currency discounts and premiums

USD/SGD : 1.3200; USD/AUD: 1.4000; AUD/SGD: 0.9429

(5) End-of day run to compute realised exchange gains/losses on FX deals that matured and post entries

Val15-4-1	Ccy	Amount	Rate	Ccy	Amount
FX Deal #5					
Contract	SGD	110,000	1.1000	USD	100,000
Book rate May 4	SGD	110,000	1.3200	USD	83,333
Gains				USD	16,667

(Purchase base currency and an increase in rate = gains in exchange)

Note: Realised gains or losses measures contract rate against book rate.

VR15-4-3	Ccy	Dr	Cr
USD LEDGER : Accounts			
Spot exchange position	USD	16,667	
Realised exchange p&l	USD		16,667

Note : Realised exchange gains or losses cause currency mismatch, or creates an open spot exchange position, in the currency which takes up the gains/losses, in this case, the USD.

(6) End-of-day run to compute unrealised exchange p&l on forward FX deals and post entries.
Not applicable. There are no outstanding FX deals.

(7) End-of-day run to compute revaluation on brought forward spot exchange positions, and post entries.
Not applicable. There are no spot exchange positions brought forward.

ASSETS & LIABILITIES AS AT MAY 4

Fig 19 Assets-Liabilities with spot exchange positions caused by deal settlement

4 May 2022	USD Ledger		SGD Ledger		AUD Ledger		Reporting SGD	
	Assets	Liabilities	Assets	Liabilities	Assets	Liabilities	Assets	Liabilities
Other Assets-Liabilities	5,000,000	5,000,000	3,000,000	3,000,000	200,000	200,000	9,788,580	9,788,580
Nostro	100,000	0	0	110,000	0	0	132,000	110,000
Spot exchange position	0	83,333	110,000	0	0	0	110,000	110,000
Fwd Exc revaluation	0	0	0	0	0	0	0	0
Profit & Loss (equity)	0	0	0	0	0	0	0	0
Unrealised Exc p&l	0	0	0	0	0	0	0	0
Realised Exchange p&l	0	16,667	0	0	0	0	0	22,000
Spot exc revaluaton p&l	0	0	0	0	0	0	0	0
TOTAL	5,100,000	5,100,000	3,110,000	3,110,000	200,000	200,000	10,030,580	10,030,580
Book rates	1.3200	1.3200	1.0000	1.0000	0.9429	0.9429		
Translated to SGD	6,732,000	6,732,000	3,110,000	3,110,000	188,580	188,580	10,030,580	10,030,580
OFF BALANCE SHEET:								
FX purchased	0	0	0	0	0	0		
FX sold	0	0	0	0	0	0		
Fwd exc position USD/SGD	0	0	0	0	0	0		
Fwd exc position USD/AUD	0	0	0	0	0	0		
Fwd exc position AUD/SGD	0	0	0	0	0	0		
	0	0	0	0	0	0		

Note:

- May 2 to May 4 shows the life cycle of a FX transaction, from inception to maturity.
- There are now spot exchange position balances carried forward. As forward deals mature, they move from the forward books into the cash books and cause currency mismatches. The mismatch positions are reflected in the spot exchange position accounts.
- Note in fig. 19 the spot exchange positions created by deal #5 on maturity cancel each other out without the need for revaluation. This is because on the date of maturity the FX deal has already been revalued and its realised exchange gains or losses accounted for. Thus the spot exchange positions caused by the maturing deals of the day do not require revaluation as the open positions cancel each other out on the day it matured.
- Revaluation will be done on the spot positions created by matured FX deals on days subsequent to the day of maturity. Thus the spot position created by FX deal #5 will require revaluation from May 5 onward as we shall see next.
- In other words, revaluation of spot exchange positions is on brought forward balances.

****

15.5 May 5 : Revaluation on spot exchange positions brought forward

Shows how spot exchange positions are revalued and how spot revaluation gains and losses are treated.

(1) Start-of-day run to reverse the unrealised exchange p&l entries of the previous day
Not applicable. No outstanding FX deals on May 4, no forward revaluation.

(2) Enter new FX transactions
Not applicable. No new transaction

(3) Post settlement entries of FX deals that matured during the day
Not applicable. No FX deals maturing.

(4) Update book-rates and currency discounts and premiums
USD/SGD : 1.3500; USD/AUD: 1.4000; AUD/SGD: 0.9643

Fig 20 Assets-Liabilities BEFORE revaluation of spot exchange positions

5 May 2022	USD Ledger		SGD Ledger		AUD Ledger		Reporting SGD	
	Assets	Liabilities	Assets	Liabilities	Assets	Liabilities	Assets	Liabilities
Other Assets-Liabilities	5,000,000	5,000,000	3,000,000	3,000,000	200,000	200,000	9,942,860	9,942,860
Nostro	100,000	0	0	110,000	0	0	135,000	110,000
Spot exchange position	0	83,333	110,000	0	0	0	110,000	112,500
Fwd Exc revaluation	0	0	0	0	0	0	0	0
Profit & Loss (equity)	0	0	0	0	0	0	0	0
Unrealised Exc p&l	0	0	0	0	0	0	0	0
Realised Exchange p&l	0	16,667	0	0	0	0	0	22,500
Spot exc revaluaton p&l	0	0	0	0	0	0	0	0
TOTAL	5,100,000	5,100,000	3,110,000	3,110,000	200,000	200,000	10,187,860	10,187,860
Book rates	1.3500	1.3500	1.0000	1.0000	0.9643	0.9643		
Translated to SGD	6,885,000	6,885,000	3,110,000	3,110,000	192,860	192,860	10,187,860	10,187,860
OFF BALANCE SHEET:								
FX purchased	0	0	0	0	0	0		
FX sold	0	0	0	0	0	0		
Fwd exc position USD/SGD	0	0	0	0	0	0		
Fwd exc position USD/AUD	0	0	0	0	0	0		
Fwd exc position AUD/SGD	0	0	0	0	0	0		
	0	0	0	0	0	0		

Note:

- Once the book-rates are updated for the day, the spot exchange balances are out of sync. They no longer eliminate on consolidation in a reporting currency.
- On an ongoing basis, banks always have opening balances in spot exchange position accounts. Thus spot exchange position revaluation is a daily affair. In our illustration, May 5 is the first time we have an opening balance in the spot position accounts.

(5) End-of day run to compute realised exchange p&l on FX deals that matured and post entries

Not applicable. No FX deals maturing.

(6) End-of-day run to compute unrealised exchange p&l on forward FX deals and post entries.

Not applicable. There are no outstanding FX deals.

(7) End-of-day run to compute revaluation on brought forward spot exchange positions, and post entries.

Val15-5-1	Ccy	Amount	Rate	Ccy	Amount
Spot exc position SGD:					
Book rate May 4	SGD	110,000	1.3200	USD	83,333
Book rate May 5	SGD	110,000	1.3500	USD	81,481
Gains				USD	1,852

(Long base currency and an increase in rate = gains in exchange)

VR15-5-1	Ccy	Dr	Cr
USD LEDGER : Accounts			
Spot exchange position	USD	1,852	
Spot exc revaluation p&l	USD		1,852

Note :

Just as for realised exchange gains or losses, revaluation of spot exchange positions cause currency mismatch, or creates an open spot exchange position, in the currency which takes up the gains/loses, in this case, the USD.

ASSETS & LIABILITIES AS AT MAY 5

Fig 20a Assets-Liabilities AFTER revaluation of spot exchange positions

5 May 2022	USD Ledger		SGD Ledger		AUD Ledger		Reporting SGD	
	Assets	Liabilities	Assets	Liabilities	Assets	Liabilities	Assets	Liabilities
Other Assets-Liabilities	5,000,000	5,000,000	3,000,000	3,000,000	200,000	200,000	9,942,860	9,942,860
Nostro	100,000	0	0	110,000	0	0	135,000	110,000
Spot exchange position	0	81,481	110,000	0	0	0	110,000	109,999
Fwd Exc revaluation	0	0	0	0	0	0	0	0
Profit & Loss (equity)	0	0	0	0	0	0	0	0
Unrealised Exc p&l	0	0	0	0	0	0	0	0
Realised Exc p&l	0	16,667	0	0	0	0	0	22,500
Exc Revaluation p&l	0	1,852	0	0	0	0	0	2,500
TOTAL	5,100,000	5,100,000	3,110,000	3,110,000	200,000	200,000	10,187,860	10,187,860
Book rates	1.3500	1.3500	1.0000	1.0000	0.9643	0.9643		
Translated to SGD	6,885,000	6,885,000	3,110,000	3,110,000	192,860	192,860	10,187,860	10,187,860
OFF BALANCE SHEET:								
FX purchased	0	0	0	0	0	0		
FX sold	0	0	0	0	0	0		
Fwd exc position USD/SGD	0	0	0	0	0	0		
Fwd exc position USD/AUD	0	0	0	0	0	0		
Fwd exc position AUD/SGD	0	0	0	0	0	0		
	0	0	0	0	0	0		

Note: After revaluation of spot exchange positions, assets-liabilities mismatch can now be eliminated on consolidation in a reporting currency. ($1 difference is due to rounding errors). Spot revaluation is performed on brought forward spot positions, not the current day's end of day balance. On an ongoing basis, all banks carry spot exchange positions all the time, thus revaluation of opening spot exchange position balances is a daily routine.

****

15.6 May 6 - May 30 No changes

For the convenience of explanation, assume from May 6 to May 30 there are no new transactions and book rate remains unchanged from May 5 throughout. There is thus no forward revaluation and spot revaluation turns up nil gains/losses since the book-rate remains unchanged. Thus the asset-liability status Fig.20a remains unchanged from May 5 to May 30.

****

15.7 May 31 Accounting period end closing of accounts

The bank system closes out all revenue and expenditure accounts to equity (Profit & Loss account) monthly.

On May 31 : FX deal #6 - Bought 300,000 USD/SGD at 1.3600 Value Aug 2.

(1) Start-of-day run to reverse the unrealised exchange p&l entries of the previous day
Not applicable. No forward revaluation on May 31.

(2) Enter new FX transactions
Deal inception - FX #6

VR15-7-1	Ccy	Dr	Cr
USD LEDGER : Accounts			
FX purchased	USD	300,000	
Forward exc position USD/SGD	USD		300,000
SGD LEDGER : Accounts			
Forward exc position USD/SGD	SGD	408,000	
FX sold	SGD		408,000

(3) Post settlement entries of FX deals that matured during the day
Not applicable. No FX deals maturing.

(4) Update book-rates and currency discounts and premiums
USD/SGD : 1.3520; USD/AUD: 1.4000; AUD/SGD: 0.9463

(5) End-of day run to compute realised exchange p&l on FX deals that matured and post entries
Not applicable. No FX deals maturing.

(6) End-of-day run to compute unrealised exchange p&l on forward FX deals and post entries.

There was only 1 deal outstanding.

Val15-7-1	Ccy	Amount	Rate	Ccy	Amount
FX Deal #6					
Contract	SGD	408,000	1.3600	USD	300,000
Expected rate Aug 2	SGD	408,000	1.3650	USD	298,901
Gains				USD	1,099

(Purchase base currency and an increase in rate = gains in exchange)

VR15-7-2	Ccy	Dr	Cr
USD LEDGER : Accounts			
Forward exchange revaluation	USD	1,099	
Unrealised Exchange p&l	USD		1,099

(7) End-of-day run to compute revaluation on brought forward spot exchange positions, and post entries.

Val15-7-2	Ccy	Amount	Rate	Ccy	Amount
Spot exc position SGD:					
Book rate May 30	SGD	110,000	1.3500	USD	81,481
Book rate May 31	SGD	110,000	1.3520	USD	81,361
Gains				USD	120

(Long base currency and an increase in rate = gains in exchange)

VR15-7-3	Ccy	Dr	Cr
USD LEDGER : Accounts			
Spot exc position	USD	120	
Spot exchange revaluation p&l	USD		120

ASSETS & LIABILITIES AS AT MAY 31 BEFORE MONTHEND CLOSING:

Fig 21 Assets-Liabilities BEFORE month end closing

31 May 2022	USD Ledger		SGD Ledger		AUD Ledger		Reporting SGD	
	Assets	Liabilities	Assets	Liabilities	Assets	Liabilities	Assets	Liabilities
Other Assets-Liabilities	5,000,000	5,000,000	3,000,000	3,000,000	200,000	200,000	9,952,860	9,952,860
Nostro	100,000	0	0	110,000	0	0	135,200	110,000
Spot exc position	0	81,361	110,000	0	0	0	110,000	110,000
Fwd revaluation	1,099	0	0	0	0	0	1,486	0
Profit & Loss (equity)	0	0	0	0	0	0	0	0
Unrealised Exc p&l	0	1,099	0	0	0	0	0	1,486
Realised Exchange p&l	0	16,667	0	0	0	0	0	22,534
Exc Revaluation p&l	0	1,972	0	0	0	0	0	2,666
TOTAL	5,101,099	5,101,099	3,110,000	3,110,000	200,000	200,000	10,199,546	10,199,546
Book rates	1.3520	1.3520	1.0000	1.0000	0.9643	0.9643		
Translated to SGD	6,896,686	6,896,686	3,110,000	3,110,000	192,860	192,860	10,199,546	10,199,546
OFF BALANCE SHEET:								
FX purchased	300,000	0	0	0	0	0		
FX sold	0	0	0	408,000	0	0		
Fwd exc position USD/SGD	0	300,000	408,000	0	0	0		
Fwd exc position USD/AUD	0	0	0	0	0	0		
Fwd exc position AUD/SGD	0	0	0	0	0	0		
	300,000	300,000	408,000	408,000	0	0		

(8) End-of-month run to close revenue/expense accounts to equity.

VR15-7-4	Ccy	Dr	Cr
USD LEDGER : Accounts			
Unrealised exchange p&l	USD	1,099	
Realised exchange p&l	USD	16,667	
Spot exchange revaluation p&l	USD	1,972	
Profit & Loss A/c	USD		19,738

How to reconcile the exchange p&l taken into equity at each month-end closing? It comprises of:

Tab15-7-1		May USD	June USD
A.	Unrealised Exchange p&l on outstanding deals as at current month end May 31 (in our illustration, there is only 1 deal - FX #6 Step [6] above)	1,099	
B.	Realised exchange p&l on FX deals that matured in current month. (In our illustration, there is only 1 deal - FX deal #5 see May 4 Step [5])	16,667	
C.	Spot exc revaluation gains on spot positions in current month (see May 5 step [7] USD1,852 + May 31 step [7] USD120	1,972	
	TOTAL	19,738	
D.	LESS Unrealised exchange p&l of outstanding deals as at previous monthend.	0	1,099
	TOTAL FOR THE MONTH	19,738	

Note :

- (D) represents the sum of unrealised exchange gains or losses of the forward deals outstanding as at monthend which have already been transferred to previous month's equity. This is the 'shadow posting' mechanism as explained in chapter 12.
- (D) is nil for May since it is the first month.
- The sum in (A) for May will be the (D) for the following month of June.
- Fig. 21a below shows the forward exchange revaluation account as at May 31 was USD1,099. The 'shadow posting' will cause this to be reversed, ie credited, out of Forward Exchange revaluation A/c and debited to Exchange P&L a/c.
- Thus the revenue account will start June 1 with a negative USD1,099. As the new forward revaluation computed for June 1 will later be shadow posted (credited) to the revenue account, the gains for the new day (Jun 1) will have USD1,099 netted off as that amount has already been transferred to equity in May.

ASSETS & LIABILITIES AS AT MAY 31 AFTER MONTH END CLOSING:

Fig 21a- Assets-Liabilities AFTER Month end closing

31 May 2022	USD Ledger		SGD Ledger		AUD Ledger		Reporting SGD	
	Assets	Liabilities	Assets	Liabilities	Assets	Liabilities	Assets	Liabilities
Other Assets-Liabilities	5,000,000	5,000,000	3,000,000	3,000,000	200,000	200,000	9,952,860	9,952,860
Nostro	100,000	0	0	110,000	0	0	135,200	110,000
Spot exc position	0	81,361	110,000	0	0	0	110,000	110,000
Fwd Exc revaluation	1,099	0	0	0	0	0	1,486	0
Profit & Loss (equity)	0	19,738	0	0	0	0	0	26,686
Unrealised exc p&l	0	0	0	0	0	0	0	0
Realised Exc p&l	0	0	0	0	0	0	0	0
Spot revaluation p&l	0	0	0	0	0	0	0	0
TOTAL	5,101,099	5,101,099	3,110,000	3,110,000	200,000	200,000	10,199,546	10,199,546
Book rates	1.3520	1.3520	1.0000	1.0000	0.9643	0.9643		
Translated to SGD	6,896,686	6,896,686	3,110,000	3,110,000	192,860	192,860	10,199,546	10,199,546
OFF BALANCE SHEET:								
FX purchased	300,000	0	0	0	0	0		
FX sold		0	0	408,000	0	0		
Fwd exc position USD/SGD	0	300,000	408,000	0	0	0		
Fwd exc position USD/AUD	0	0	0	0	0	0		
Fwd exc position AUD/SGD	0	0	0	0	0	0		
	300,000	300,000	408,000	408,000	0	0		

****

15.8 June 1 : Post month-end status

The purpose in this illustration is to show how the unrealised exchange p&l account at the beginning of a new accounting period is affected by the shadow posting technique, which basically deducts the amount already closed off to the previous month from the current day's gains or loss.

New deal : Same day value FX Deal #7 Sell 400,000 USD/AUD at 1.4400 value Jun 2.

(1) Start-of-day run to reverse entries of the previous day for unrealised exchange p&l on forward FX deals.

VR15-8-1	Ccy	Dr	Cr
USD LEDGER : Accounts			
Unrealised exchange p&l	USD	1,099	
Forward exchange revaluation	USD		1,099

(2) Enter new FX transactins

VR15-8-2	Ccy	Dr	Cr
USD LEDGER : Accounts			
Forward exc position USD/AUD	USD	400,000	
FX sold	USD		400,000
AUD LEDGER : Accounts			
FX purchased	AUD	576,000	
Forward exc position USD/AUD	AUD		576,000

(3) Post settlement entries of FX deals that matured during the day

In respect of FX Deal #7

VR15-8-3	Ccy	Dr	Cr
USD LEDGER : Accounts			
FX sold	USD	400,000	
Forward exc position USD/AUD	USD		400,000
Spot exchange position	USD	400,000	
Nostro	USD		400,000
AUD LEDGER : Accounts			
Forward exc position USD/AUD	AUD	576,000	
FX purchased	AUD		576,000
Nostro	AUD	576,000	
Spot exchange position	AUD		576,000

(4) Update book-rates and currency discounts and premiums

USD/SGD : 1.3600; USD/AUD: 1.4500; AUD/SGD: 0.93793

(5) End-of day run to compute realised exchange p&l on FX deals that matured and post entries

Val15-8-1	Ccy	Amount	Rate	Ccy	Amount
FX deal #7					
Contract	AUD	576,000	1.4400	USD	400,000
Book rate	AUD	576,000	1.4500	USD	397,241
Loss				USD	2,759

(Sell base currency and an increase in rate = loss in exchange)

VR15-8-4	Ccy	Dr	Cr
USD LEDGER : Accounts			
Realised Exchange p&l	USD	2,759	
Spot exchange position	USD		2,759

(6) End-of-day to compute unrealised exchange p&l on forward FX deals and post entries.

There is only 1 deal outstanding

Val15-8-2	Ccy	Amount	Rate	Ccy	Amount
FX deal #6					
Contract	SGD	408,000	1.3600	USD	300,000
Expected rate for Aug 2	SGD	408,000	1.3675	USD	298,355
Gains				USD	1,645

(Purchase base currency and an increase in rate = gains in exchange)

VR15-8-5	Ccy	Dr	Cr
USD LEDGER : Accounts			
Forward exchange revaluation	USD	1,645	
Unrealised Exchange p&l	USD		1,645

(7) End-of-day run to compute revaluation on brought forward spot exchange positions, and post entries.

Val15-8-3	Ccy	Amount	Rate	Ccy	Amount
Spot exch position SGD:					
Book rate May 31	SGD	110,000	1.3520	USD	81,361
Book rate Jun 1	SGD	110,000	1.3600	USD	80,882
Gains				USD	479

(Purchase base currency and an increase in rate = gains in exchange)

VR15-8-6	Ccy	Dr	Cr
USD LEDGER : Accounts			
Spot exchange position	USD	479	
Spot exchange revaluation p&l	USD		479

Note : There is no revaluation of AUD spot exchange position created by FX Deal #7 today. This will be subject to spot revaluation Jun 2 onward.

ASSETS & LIABILITIES AS AT JUN 1:

Fig 22 Assets-Liabilities new month

1 June 2022	USD Ledger		SGD Ledger		AUD Ledger		Reporting SGD	
	Assets	Liabilities	Assets	Liabilities	Assets	Liabilities	Assets	Liabilities
Other Assets-Liabilities	5,000,000	5,000,000	3,000,000	3,000,000	200,000	200,000	9,987,586	9,987,586
Nostro	0	300,000	0	110,000	576,000	0	540,248	518,000
Spot exc position	316,359	0	110,000	0	0	576,000	540,248	540,248
Fwd Exc revaluation	1,645	0	0	0	0	0	2,237	0
Profit & Loss (equity)	0	19,738	0	0	0	0	0	26,844
Realised Exc p&l	2,759	0	0	0	0	0	3,752	0
Unrealised Exc p&l	0	546	0	0	0	0	0	743
Spot revaluation p&l	0	479	0	0	0	0	0	651
TOTAL	5,320,763	5,320,763	3,110,000	3,110,000	776,000	776,000	11,074,071	11,074,071
Book rates	1.3600	1.3600	1.0000	1.0000	0.93793	0.93793		
Translated to SGD	7,236,238	7,236,238	3,110,000	3,110,000	727,834	727,834	11,074,071	11,074,071
OFF BALANCE SHEET:								
FX purchased	300,000	0	0	0	0	0		
FX sold		0	0	408,000	0	0		
Fwd exc position USD/SGD	0	300,000	408,000	0	0	0		
Fwd exc position USD/AUD	0	0	0	0	0	0		
Fwd exc position AUD/SGD	0	0	0	0	0	0		
	300,000	300,000	408,000	408,000	0	0		

Note: The unrealised exchange p&l from forward revaluation is a gain of USD1,645 but the statement shows only USD546. The ledger explains.

AC15-8-1		A/c : Unrealised Exc p&l	Dr	Cr	Balance
Date	Ref	Details	USD	USD	USD
May 31		Forward FX deal revaluation		1,099	1,099
May 31		Transfer to P&L	-1,099		0
Jun 1		Reversal of May 31	-1,099		-1,099
Jun 1		Forward FX deal revaluation		1,645	546

This is due to the shadow posting technique of reversing the previous day's entries out of the suspense or provision account (Forward exchange revaluation a/c). On May 31 the forward exchange revaluation was a gains of USD1,099. On Jun 1 this is reversed out of the provision account back to debit of Unrealised exchange p&l account which now shows a net credit of USD 546 (USD1,645- USD1,099). What this means is of the USD1,645 forward revaluation gains on Jun 1, USD1,099 has already been taken up in May's profit & loss account after the accounting period closing.

****

15.9 June 2 : Typical Day accounting tasks

New deals :

- **Deal #8 Sell 500,000 USD/AUD at 1.4405 for value Jun 2.**
- **Deal #9 Sell 1,000,000 USD/AUD at 1.4410 for value Jul 3.**

Banks are active in foreign exchange market. Each day it has new deals written, deals up for settlement, and a vast number of outstanding forward FX contracts. On a typical day, all the 7 steps of accounting tasks would be accomplished. Let's take a look at a typical day.

(1) Start-of-day run to reverse entries of the previous day for unrealised exchange p&l on forward FX deals.

VR15-9-1	Ccy	Dr	Cr
USD LEDGER : Accounts			
Unrealised Exchange p&l	USD	1,645	
Forward exchange revaluation	USD		1,645

(2) Enter new FX transactions

Deal inception FX Deal #8 & FX #9

VR15-9-2	Ccy	Dr	Cr
USD LEDGER : Accounts			
Forward exc position USD/AUD	USD	500,000	
FX sold FX #8	USD		500,000
Forward exc position USD/AUD	USD	1,000,000	
FX sold FX #9	USD		1,000,000
AUD LEDGER : Accounts			
FX purchased FX #8	AUD	720,250	
Forward exc position USD/AUD	AUD		720,250
Fx purchased FX #9	AUD	1,441,000	
Forward exc position USD/AUD	AUD		1,441,000

(3) Post settlement entries of FX deals that matured during the day

Deal matured FX Deal #8

VR15-9-3	Ccy	Dr	Cr
USD LEDGER : Accounts			
FX sold	USD	500,000	
Forward exc position USD/AUD	USD		500,000
Spot exc position	USD	500,000	
Nostro	USD		500,000
AUD LEDGER : Accounts			
Forward exc position USD/AUD	AUD	720,250	
FX purchased	AUD		720,250
Nostro	AUD	720,250	
Spot exc position	AUD		720,250

(4) Update book-rates and currency discounts and premiums

USD/SGD: 1.3650; USD/AUD: 1.4550; AUD/SGD: 0.938144

(5) End-of-day run to compute realised exchange p&l on FX deals that matured and post entries

Val15-9-1	Ccy	Amount	Rate	Ccy	Amount
FX deal #8					
Contract	AUD	720,250	1.4405	USD	500,000
Book rate	AUD	720,250	1.4550	USD	495,017
Loss				USD	4,983

(Sell base currency and an increase in rate = loss in exchange)

VR15-9-4	Ccy	Dr	Cr
USD LEDGER : Accounts			
Realised Exchange p&l	USD	4,983	
Spot exchange position	USD		4,983

(6) End-of-day run to compute unrealised exchange p&l on forward FX deals and post entries.

Performed on outstanding forward FX deals - FX #6 and FX #9

Val15-9-2	Ccy	Amount	Rate	Ccy	Amount
FX deal #6					
Contract	SGD	408,000	1.3600	USD	300,000
Expected rate Aug 2	SGD	408,000	1.3700	USD	297,810
Gains				USD	2,190

(Purchase base currency and an increase in rate =gains in exchange)

VR15-9-5	Ccy	Dr	Cr
USD LEDGER : Accounts			
Forward exchange revaluation	USD	2,190	
Unrealised Exchange p&l	USD		2,190

Val15-9-3	Ccy	Amount	Rate	Ccy	Amount
FX deal #9					
Contract	AUD	1,441,000	1.4410	USD	1,000,000
Expected rate Jul 2	AUD	1,441,000	1.4400	USD	1,000,694
Gains				USD	-694

(Sold base currency and a decrease in rate = gain in exchange)

VR15-9-6	Ccy	Dr	Cr
USD LEDGER : Accounts			
Forward exchange revaluation	USD	694	
Unrealised Exchange p&l	USD		694

(7) End-of-day run to compute revaluation on brought forward balances in spot exchange positions, and post entries.

Worth repeating—spot revaluation is performed on the brought forward balances.

Val15-9-4	Ccy	Amount	Rate	Ccy	Amount
Spot exc position SGD					
Book rate Jun 1	SGD	110,000	1.3600	USD	80,882
Book rate Jun 2	SGD	110,000	1.3650	USD	80,586
Gains				USD	296

(Long base currency and an increase in rate =gains in exchange)

VR15-9-7	Ccy	Dr	Cr
USD LEDGER : Accounts			
Spot exchange position	USD	296	
Spot exchange revaluation p&l	USD		296

Val15-9-5	Ccy	Amount	Rate	Ccy	Amount
Spot exc position AUD					
Book rate Jun 1	AUD	576,000	1.4500	USD	397,241
Book rate Jun 2	AUD	576,000	1.4550	USD	395,876
Loss				USD	1,365

(Short base currency and an increase in rate =loss in exchange)

VR15-9-8	Ccy	Dr	Cr
USD LEDGER : Accounts			
Spot exchange revaluation p&l	USD	1,365	
Spot exchange position	USD		1,365

ASSETS & LIABILITIES AS AT JUN 2:

Fig 23 Assets-Liabilities after a typical end of day

2 June 2022	USD Ledger		SGD Ledger		AUD Ledger		Reporting SGD	
	Assets	Liabilities	Assets	Liabilities	Assets	Liabilities	Assets	Liabilities
Other Assets-Liabilities	5,000,000	5,000,000	3,000,000	3,000,000	200,000	200,000	10,012,629	10,012,629
Nostro	0	800,000	0	110,000	1,296,250	0	1,216,069	1,202,000
Spot exchange position	810,307	0	110,000	0	0	1,296,250	1,216,069	1,216,069
Fwd Exc revaluation	2,884	0	0	0	0	0	3,937	0
P&L equity	0	19,738	0	0	0	0	0	26,942
Unrealised Exc p&l	0	1,785	0	0	0	0	0	2,437
Realised Exc p&l	7,742	0	0	0	0	0	10,568	0
Spot exc revaluation p&l	590	0	0	0	0	0	805	0
TOTAL	5,821,523	5,821,523	3,110,000	3,110,000	1,496,250	1,496,250	12,460,077	12,460,077
Book rates	1.3650	1.3650	1.0000	1.0000	0.938144	0.938144		
Translated to SGD	7,946,379	7,946,379	3,110,000	3,110,000	1,403,698	1,403,698	12,460,077	12,460,077
OFF BALANCE SHEET:								
FX purchased		1,000,000	0	0	1,441,000	0		
FX sold	300,000	0	0	408,000	0	0		
Fwd exc position USD/SGD	0	300,000	408,000	0	0	0		
Fwd exc position USD/AUD	1,000,000		0	0	0	1,441,000		
Fwd exc position AUD/SGD	0	0	0	0	0	0		
	1,300,000	1,300,000	408,000	408,000	1,441,000	1,441,000		

****

15.10 USD Ledger

AC15-10-1		A/c : FX purchased	Dr	Cr	Balance
Date	Ref	Details	USD	USD	USD
May 2		Deal inception - FX #5	-100,000		-100,000
May 4		Deal settlement - FX #5		100,000	0
May 31		Deal inception - FX #6	-300,000		-300,000

AC15-10-2		A/c : FX sold	Dr	Cr	Balance
Date	Ref	Details	USD	USD	USD
Jun 1		Deal inception - Fx #7		400,000	400,000
Jun 1		Deal settlement - FX #7	-400,000		0
Jun 2		Deal inception FX #8		500,000	500,000
Jun 2		Deal inception FX #9		1,000,000	1,500,000
Jun 2		Deal settlement FX 8	-500,000		1,000,000

AC15-10-3		A/c : Fwd Exc Position USD/SGD	Dr	Cr	Balance
Date	Ref	Details	USD	USD	USD
May 2		Deal inception - FX #5		100,000	100,000
May 4		Deal settlement - FX #5	-100,000		0
May 31		Deal inception - FX #6		300,000	300,000

AC15-10-4		A/c : Fwd Exc Position USD/AUD	Dr	Cr	Balance
Date	Ref	Details	USD	USD	USD
Jun 1		Deal inception - FX#7	-400,000		-400,000
Jun 1		Deal settlement - FX #7		400,000	0
Jun 2		FX deal inception FX #8	-500,000		-500,000
Jun 2		FX deal inception FX #9	-1,000,000		-1,500,000
Jun 2		Deal settlement FX #8		500,000	-1,000,000

AC15-10-5		A/c : Nostro	Dr	Cr	Balance
Date	Ref	Details	USD	USD	USD
May 4		Deal settlement FX #5	-100,000		-100,000
Jun 1		Deal settlement FX #7		400,000	300,000
Jun 2		Deal settlement FX #8		500,000	800,000

AC15-10-6		A/c : Spot exchange position	Dr	Cr	Balance
Date	Ref	Details	USD	USD	USD
May 4		Deal settlement - FX #5		100,000	100,000
May 4		Realised exchange - FX #5	-16,667		83,333
May 5		Spot exc revaluation SGD	-1,852		81,481
May 31		Spot exc revaluation SGD	-120		81,361
Jun 1		Spot exc revaluation SGD	-479		80,882
Jun 1		Deal settlement - FX #7	-400,000		-319,118
Jun 2		Realised FX p&l - FX #7		2,759	-316,359
Jun 2		Spot exc revaluation SGD	-296		-316,655
Jun 2		Deal settlement FX #8	-500,000		-816,655
Jun 2		Realised FX p&l FX #8		4,983	-811,672
Jun 2		Spot exc revaluation AUD		1,365	-810,307

AC15-10-7		A/c : Forward exc revaluation	Dr	Cr	Balance
Date	Ref	Details	USD	USD	USD
May 2		Forward FX deal revaluation	-13,386		-13,386
May 3		Reversal of May 2		13,386	0
May 3		Forward FX deal revaluation	-14,062		-14,062
May 4		Reversal of May 3		14,062	0
May 31		Forward FX deal revaluation	-1,099		-1,099
Jun 1		Reversal of May 31		1,099	0
Jun 1		Forward FX deal revaluation	-1,545		-1,645
Jun 2		Reversal of Jun 1		1,645	0
Jun 2		Forward FX deal revaluation	-2,190		-2,190
Jun 2		Forward FX deal revaluatin	-694		-2,884

AC15-10-8		A/c : Profit & Loss (equity)	Dr	Cr	Balance
Date	Ref	Details	USD	USD	USD
May 31		Unrealised Exc p&l May		1,099	1,099
May 31		Realised Exc p&l May		16,667	17,776
May 31		Exc revaluation p&l May		1,972	19,738

AC15-10-9		A/c : Unrealised Exc p&l	Dr	Cr	Balance
Date	Ref	Details	USD	USD	USD
May 2		Forward FX deal revaluation		13	13
May 3		Reversal of May 2	-13,386		0
May 3		Forward FX deal revaluation		14,062	14,062
May 4		Reversal of May 3	-14,062		0
May 31		Forward FX deal revaluation		1,099	1,099
May 31		Transfer to P&L	-1,099		0
Jun 1		Reversal of May 31	-1,099		-1,099
Jun 1		Forward FX deal revaluation		1,645	546
Jun 2		Reversal of Jun 1	-1,645		-1,099
Jun 2		Forward FX deal revaluation		2,190	1,091
Jun 2		Forward FX deal revaluation		694	1,785

AC15-10-10		A/c : Unrealised Exc p&l	Dr	Cr	Balance
Date	Ref	Details	USD	USD	USD
May 4		Realised exchange FX#5		16,667	16,667
May 31		Transfer to P&L	-16,667		0
Jun 1		Realised exchange FX #7	-2,759		-2,759
Jun 2		Realised exchange FX #8	-4,983		-7,742

AC15-10-11		A/c : Unrealised Exc p&l	Dr	Cr	Balance
Date	Ref	Details	USD	USD	USD
May 5		Spot exc revaluation SGD		1,852	1,852
May 31		Spot exc revaluation SGD		120	1,972
May 31		Transferred to P&L	-1,972		0
Jun 1		Spot exc revaluation SGD		479	479
Jun 2		Spot exc revaluation SGD		296	775
Jun 2		Spot exc revaluation AUD	-1,365		-590

****

15.11 SGD Ledger

AC15-11-1		A/c : FX purchased	Dr	Cr	Balance
Date	Ref	Details	SGD	SGD	SGD
May 2		Deal inception - FX #5	-100,000		-100,000
May 4		Deal settlement - FX #5		100,000	0
May 31		Deal inception - FX #6	-300,000		-300,000

AC15-11-2		A/c : FX sold	Dr	Cr	Balance
Date	Ref	Details	SGD	SGD	SGD
Jun 1		Deal inception - Fx #7		400,000	400,000
Jun 1		Deal settlement - FX #7	-400,000		0
Jun 2		Deal inception FX #8		500,000	500,000
Jun 2		Deal inception FX #9		1,000,000	1,500,000
Jun 2		Deal settlement FX 8	-500,000		1,000,000

AC15-11-3		A/c : Fwd Exc Position USD/SGD	Dr	Cr	Balance
Date	Ref	Details	SGD	SGD	SGD
May 2		Deal inception - FX #5		100,000	100,000
May 4		Deal settlement - FX #5	-100,000		0
May 31		Deal inception - FX #6		300,000	300,000

AC15-11-4		A/c : Fwd Exc Position USD/AUD	Dr	Cr	Balance
Date	Ref	Details	SGD	SGD	SGD
Jun 1		Deal inception - FX#7	-400,000		-400,000
Jun 1		Deal settlement - FX #7		400,000	0
Jun 2		FX deal inception FX #8	-500,000		-500,000
Jun 2		FX deal inception FX #9	-1,000,000		-1,500,000
Jun 2		Deal settlement FX #8		500,000	-1,000,000

AC15-11-5		A/c : Nostro	Dr	Cr	Balance
Date	Ref	Details	SGD	SGD	SGD
May 4		Deal settlement FX #5	-100,000		-100,000
Jun 1		Deal settlement FX #7		400,000	300,000
Jun 2		Deal settlement FX #8		500,000	800,000

AC15-11-6		A/c : Spot exchange position	Dr	Cr	Balance
Date	Ref	Details	SGD	SGD	SGD
May 4		Deal settlement - FX #5		100,000	100,000
May 4		Realised exchange - FX #5	-16,667		83,333
May 5		Spot exc revaluation SGD	-1,852		81,481
May 31		Spot exc revaluation SGD	-120		81,361
Jun 1		Spot exc revaluation SGD	-479		80,882
Jun 1		Deal settlement - FX #7	-400,000		-319,118
Jun 2		Realised FX p&l - FX #7		2,759	-316,359
Jun 2		Spot exc revaluation SGD	-296		-316,655
Jun 2		Deal settlement FX #8	-500,000		-816,655
Jun 2		Realised FX p&l FX #8		4,983	-811,672
Jun 2		Spot exc revaluation AUD		1,365	-810,307

AC15-11-7		A/c : Forward exc revaluation	Dr	Cr	Balance
Date	Ref	Details	SGD	SGD	SGD
May 2		Forward FX deal revaluation	-13,386		-13,386
May 3		Reversal of May 2		13,386	0
May 3		Forward FX deal revaluation	-14,062		-14,062
May 4		Reversal of May 3		14,062	0
May 31		Forward FX deal revaluation	-1,099		-1,099
Jun 1		Reversal of May 31		1,099	0
Jun 1		Forward FX deal revaluation	-1,545		-1,645
Jun 2		Reversal of Jun 1		1,645	0
Jun 2		Forward FX deal revaluation	-2,190		-2,190
Jun 2		Forward FX deal revaluatin	-694		-2,884

AC15-11-8		A/c : Profit & Loss (equity)	Dr	Cr	Balance
Date	Ref	Details	SGD	SGD	SGD
May 31		Unrealised Exc p&l May		1,099	1,099
May 31		Realised Exc p&l May		16,667	17,776
May 31		Exc revaluation p&l May		1,972	19,738

AC15-11-9		A/c : Profit & Loss (equity)	Dr	Cr	Balance
Date	Ref	Details	SGD	SGD	SGD
May 2		Forward FX deal revaluation		13	13
May 3		Reversal of May 2	-13,386		0
May 3		Forward FX deal revaluation		14,062	14,062
May 4		Reversal of May 3	-14,062		0
May 31		Forward FX deal revaluation		1,099	1,099
May 31		Transfer to P&L	-1,099		0
Jun 1		Reversal of May 31	-1,099		-1,099
Jun 1		Forward FX deal revaluation		1,645	546
Jun 2		Reversal of Jun 1	-1,645		-1,099
Jun 2		Forward FX deal revaluation		2,190	1,091
Jun 2		Forward FX deal revaluation		694	1,785

AC15-11-10		A/c : Realised Exc p&l	Dr	Cr	Balance
Date	Ref	Details	SGD	SGD	SGD
May 4		Realised exchange FX#5		16,667	16,667
May 31		Transfer to P&L	-16,667		0
Jun 1		Realised exchange FX #7	-2,759		-2,759
Jun 2		Realised exchange FX #8	-4,983		-7,742

AC15-11-11		A/c : Spot Exc Revaluation p&l	Dr	Cr	Balance
Date	Ref	Details	SGD	SGD	SGD
May 5		Spot exc revaluation SGD		1,852	1,852
May 31		Spot exc revaluation SGD		120	1,972
May 31		Transferred to P&L	-1,972		0
Jun 1		Spot exc revaluation SGD		479	479
Jun 2		Spot exc revaluation SGD		296	775
Jun 2		Spot exc revaluation AUD	-1,365		-590

****

15.12 AUD Ledger

AC15-12-1		A/c : FX purchased	Dr	Cr	Balance
Date	Ref	Details	AUD	AUD	AUD
Jun 2		Deal inception - FX #7	-576,000		-576,000
Jun 2		Deal settlement - FX #7		576,000	0
Jun 2		Deal inception FX #8	-720,250		-720,250
Jun 2		Deal inception FX #9	-1,441,000		-2,161,250
Jun 2		Deal settlement FX #8		720,250	-1,441,000

AC15-12-2		A/c: Fwd Exc Position USD/AUD	Dr	Cr	Balance
Date	Ref	Details	AUD	AUD	AUD
Jun 2		Deal inception - FX #7		576,000	576,000
Jun 2		Deal settlement - FX #7	-576,000		0
Jun 2		Deal inception FX #8		720,250	720,250
Jun 2		Deal incetion FX #9		1,441,000	2,161,250
Jun 2		Deal settlement FX #8	-720,250		1,441,000

AC15-12-3		A/c: Nostro	Dr	Cr	Balance
Date	Ref	Details	AUD	AUD	AUD
Jun 2		Deal settlement FX #7	-576,000		-576,000
Jun 2		Deal settlement FX #8	-720,250		-1,296,250

AC15-12-4		A/c: Spot Exchange Position	Dr	Cr	Balance
Date	Ref	Details	AUD	AUD	AUD
Jun 2		Deal settlement - FX #7		576,000	576,000
Jun 2		Deal settlement FX #8		720,250	1,296,250

****

15.13 Review of daily activities

1. In a multi-currency accounting system, a separate self-balancing ledger is used for each currency.

2. All transactions are recognised and recorded in it's own currency ledger.

3. A transaction in any currency alone involves only compensating changes in the assets and liabilities of one currency. Such transactions create no spot exchange positions, and have no exchange p&l implication. For example, the purchase of some Yen bonds results in a decrease in Yen Nostro account balances and an increase in the Yen Securities account. A disposal of same securities involves reverse entries in the two accounts in the Yen ledger. There is thus no exchange revaluation involved in the acquisition or disposal thereof.

4. A book base currency must first be established. This is the currency with a value of '1' in relation to all other currencies. The other currencies are considered as 'other' currencies. Book base currency is essential to enable currency consolidated reporting.

5. Only foreign exchange transactions impact 2 different currency ledgers with implications for exchange gains or losses.

6. Forward exchange deals that have not yet matured are revalued (marked-to-market) daily and unrealised gains or losses are recognised. This is calculated by comparing the contracted rate to a computed rate in the future date of settlement.

7. Forward revaluation gains or losses do not affect spot exchange position accounts.

9. When a foreign exchange deal matures, its settlement moves the transaction from off-balance sheet into the real balance sheet causing cashflow imbalance in 2 currency ledgers. One currency pays and the other receives. The asset-liability mismatch is balanced by the use of mirror accounts in each currency called spot exchange position accounts.

10. Matured deals are computed for their realised gains or losses by comparing contracted rates to the book-rate on the date of settlement.

11. Spot exchange position revaluation is done by taking the brought forward balance in the spot exchange position accounts in each foreign currency ledger and comparing them to the book rate. The daily spot exchange position gains or losses are recognised.

12. The spot exchange position accounts are revalued daily so that these mirror accounts are zerorised when consolidated in any reporting currency. Revaluation of the spot exchange position accounts is in effect a translation of the various currency assets and liabilities done on a net basis.

13. When all currency ledgers are consolidated in a reporting currency, spot exchange position accounts are extinguished.

14. Realised exchange and spot exchange position revaluation gains or losses create spot positions in the currency in which the gains or losses are taken up.

15. Exchange gains or losses may be booked in any currency. In our example, it is taken up in the book base currency, the USD. The significant point is that whichever currency takes the gains or losses, it creates a long position when it is a loss, and a short position when it is a gain, in the currency which takes up the exchange difference.

15. Which currency to use to book exchange gains or losses has potential profit and loss implications. The decision should be made by Treasury management rather than by accountants.

16. Foreign exchange gains or losses are segregated into (i) unrealised FX p&l, (ii) realised FX p&l and (iii) spot exchange revaluation p&l. This supports local reporting where tax regimes may treat these income differently.

****

16. Which currency to book the exchange gains or losses

In the illustrations so far, exchange gains or losses are taken in the book base currency. There is strategic and economic argument for this since banks' business is substantially in this currency.

Accounting standards require exchange gains or losses to be taken up in the book base currency. Cross currency pairs without a book base currency require consideration of which currency should book exchange gains and losses.

- For profit centre accounting purposes, banks may want true currency profit & loss.
- An exchange gain or loss creates a spot exchange position in the currency in which it is booked. Thus the decision of which currency to book exchange gains or loss has a profit & loss implication.
- Booking the gains or losses in a currency not involved in the FX transaction is not consistent with the matching principle.

__Cross rates and splitting of exchange gains and losses__

To illustrate, let's look at the situation where the exchange gains or losses in a cross currency pair is split 50-50 between the two currencies.

Suppose the bank's assets-liabilities is like this

Fig 24 Assets-Liabilities BEFORE FX deal

	USD Ledger		SGD Ledger		AUD Ledger		Reporting USD	
	Assets	Liabilities	Assets	Liabilities	Assets	Liabilities	Assets	Liabilities
Other assets-liabilities	3,000,000	3,000,000	2,000,000	2,000,000	1,000,000	1,000,000	5,175,926	5,175,926
Nostro	0	0	0	0	0	0	0	0
Spot exchange position	0	0	0	0	0	0	0	0
Fwd Exc revaluation	0	0	0	0	0	0	0	0
P&L equity	0	0	0	0	0	0	0	0
Unrealised exchange p&l	0	0	0	0	0	0	0	0
Unrealised exchange p&l	0	0	0	0	0	0	0	0
Spot exc revaluation p&l	0	0	0	0	0	0	0	0
TOTAL	3,000,000	3,000,000	2,000,000	2,000,000	1,000,000	1,000,000	5,175,926	5,175,926
Book rates	1.0000	1.0000	1.3500	1.3500	1.4400	1.4400		
Translated to USD	3,000,000	3,000,000	1,481,481	1,481,481	694,444	694,444	5,175,926	5,175,926

Suppose this FX deal was done :

FX deal # 10 : Sold 500,000 AUD/SGD at 0.9300 same day value.

Book rates for Day 1 : AUD 1.4400; SGD 1.3500 (AUD/SGD=0.9375)

(1) Settlement entries :

VR16-1	Ccy	Dr	Cr
<u>**AUD LEDGER : Accounts**</u>			
Spot exc position	AUD	500,000	
Nostro	AUD		500,000
<u>**SGD LEDGER : Accounts**</u>			
Nostro	SGD	465,000	
Spot exc position	SGD		465,000

(2) Realised exchange gains/loss and entries :

<u>Val16-1</u>	Ccy	Amount	Rate	Ccy	Amount
<u>FX deal #10</u>					
Contract	SGD	465,000	0.9300	AUD	500,000
Book rate	SGD	465,000	0.9375	AUD	496,000
Loss				AUD	4,000
Share of loss in AUD 50%				AUD	2,000
Share of loss in SGD 50%	AUD	2,000	0.9375	SGD	1,875

(Sell base currency and an increase in rate = loss in exchange)

VR16-2	Ccy	Dr	Cr
<u>**AUD LEDGER : Accounts**</u>			
Realised Exchange p&l	AUD	2,000	
Spot exchange position	AUD		2,000
<u>**SGD LEDGER : Accounts**</u>			
Realised Exchange p&l	SGD	1,875	
Spot exchange position	SGD		1,875

Recognising exchange gains and losses in the 'other currencies' creates spot exchange positions in the relevant currencies, in this case, SGD and AUD.

Fig. 25 Assets-Liabilities after settlement on Day 1 (Gains/loss taken up in cross currencies)								
	USD Ledger		SGD Ledger		AUD Ledger		Reporting USD	
	Assets	Liabilities	Assets	Liabilities	Assets	Liabilities	Assets	Liabilities
Other Assets-Liabilities	3,000,000	3,000,000	2,000,000	2,000,000	1,000,000	1,000,000	5,175,926	5,175,926
Nostro	0	0	465,000	0	0	500,000	344,444	347,222
Spot exchange position	0	0	0	466,875	498,000	0	345,833	345,833
Fwd Exc revaluation	0	0	0	0	0	0	0	0
P&L equity	0	0	0	0	0	0	0	0
Realised Exc p&l	0	0	1,875	0	2,000	0	2,778	0
Unrealised Exc p&l	0	0	0	0	0	0	0	0
Spot exc revaluation p&l	0	0	0	0	0	0	0	0
TOTAL	3,000,000	3,000,000	2,466,875	2,466,875	1,500,000	1,500,000	5,868,981	5,868,981
Book rates	1.0000	1.0000	1.3500	1.3500	1.44000	1.44000		
Translated to USD	3,000,000	3,000,000	1,827,315	1,827,315	1,041,667	1,041,667	5,868,981	5,868,981

Book rates for day 2 : AUD 1.4550; SGD 1.3700 (AUD/SGD=0.948097)

(3) There are no other transactions. Rates have changed for Day 2, so spot exchange position balances brought forward need to be revalued.

Val16-2	Ccy	Amount	Rate	Ccy	Amount
Spot exc position SGD					
Book rate Jun 1	SGD	466,875	1.3500	USD	345,833
Book rate Jun 2	SGD	466,875	1.3700	USD	340,785
Loss				USD	5,048

(Short base currency and an increase in rate = loss in exchange)

	Ccy	Amount	Rate	Ccy	Amount
Spot exc position AUD					
Book rate Jun 1	AUD	498,000	1.4400	USD	345,833
Book rate Jun 2	AUD	498,000	1.4550	USD	342,268
Gains				USD	3,565

(Long base currency and an increase in rate =gain in exchange)

VR16-3	Ccy	Dr	Cr
USD LEDGER : Accounts			
Spot exc revaluation p&l	USD	1,483	
Spot exchange position	USD		1,483

Note that spot exchange position revaluation is a calibration with the book base currency USD. It creates spot exchange position in only the book base currency. A net loss of USD1,483 (5,048-3,565) is recognised.

Fig. 26 Assets-Liabilities after revaluation on Day 2 (Gains/loss taken up in cross currencies)

	USD Ledger		SGD Ledger		AUD Ledger		Reporting USD	
	Assets	Liabilities	Assets	Liabilities	Assets	Liabilities	Assets	Liabilities
Other Assets-Liabilities	3,000,000	3,000,000	2,000,000	2,000,000	1,000,000	1,000,000	5,147,139	5,147,139
Nostro	0	0	465,000	0	0	500,000	339,416	343,643
Spot exchange position	0	1,483	0	466,875	498,000	0	342,268	342,268
Fwd Exc revaluation	0	0	0	0	0	0	0	0
P&L equity	0	0	0	0	0	0	0	0
Realised Exc p&l	0	0	1,875	0	2,000	0	2,743	0
Unrealised Exc p&l	0	0	0	0	0	0	0	0
Spot exc revaluation p&l	1,483	0	0	0	0	0	1,483	0
TOTAL	3,001,483	3,001,483	2,466,875	2,466,875	1,500,000	1,500,000	5,833,050	5,833,050
Book rates	1.0000	1.0000	1.3700	1.3700	1.45500	1.45500		
Translated to USD	3,001,483	3,001,483	1,800,639	1,800,639	1,030,928	1,030,928	5,833,050	5,833,050

Cross rates and taking gains and losses in the book base (functional) currency

Now let's see what happens if IAS21 is complied and the exchange p&l is taken up in the functional currency USD which is used as the book base currency.

Let's first work on the realised exchange p&l on Day 1 deal settlement

Val16-3	Ccy	Amount	Rate	Ccy	Amount		USD
FX deal #10							
Contract	SGD	465,000	0.9300	AUD	500,000		
Book rate	SGD	465,000	0.9375	AUD	496,000		
Loss				AUD	4,000	1.4400	2,778
(Sell base currency and an increase in rate = loss in exchange)							
Contract	AUD	500,000	0.9300	SGD	465,000		
Book rate	AUD	500,000	0.9375	SGD	468,750		
Loss				AUD	-3,750	1.3500	-2,778
(Sell base currency and an increase in rate = loss in exchange)							

Note : From either currency's perspective, the exchange gains or losses is still the same in book base currency terms. Entries are:

VR16-4	Ccy	Dr	Cr
USD LEDGER : Accounts			
Realised Exchange p&l	USD	2,778	
Spot exchange position	USD		2,778

Fig. 27 Asset-liability after settlement on Day 1 (Gains/loss taken up in book base currency)

	USD Ledger		SGD Ledger		AUD Ledger		Reporting USD	
	Assets	Liabilities	Assets	Liabilities	Assets	Liabilities	Assets	Liabilities
Other Assets-Liabilities	3,000,000	3,000,000	2,000,000	2,000,000	1,000,000	1,000,000	5,175,926	5,175,926
Nostro	0	0	465,000	0	0	500,000	344,444	347,222
Spot exchange position	0	2,778	0	465,000	500,000	0	347,222	347,222
Fwd Exc revaluation	0	0	0	0	0	0	0	0
P&L equity	0	0	0	0	0	0	0	0
Realised Exc p&l	2,778	0	0	0	0	0	2,778	0
Unrealised Exc p&l	0	0	0	0	0	0	0	0
Spot exc revaluation p&l	0	0	0	0	0	0	0	0
TOTAL	3,002,778	3,002,778	2,465,000	2,465,000	1,500,000	1,500,000	5,870,371	5,870,371
Book rates	1.0000	1.0000	1.3500	1.3500	1.44000	1.44000		
Translated to USD	3,002,778	3,002,778	1,825,926	1,825,926	1,041,667	1,041,667	5,870,371	5,870,371

Next let's look at spot exchange position revaluation conducted on Day 2.

Val16-4	Ccy	Amount	Rate	Ccy	Amount
Spot exch position SGD:					
Book rate Day 1	SGD	465,000	1.3500	USD	344,444
Book rate Day 2	SGD	465,000	1.3700	USD	339,416
					5,028
(Short base currency and an increase in rate = loss in exchange)					
Spot exch position AUD					
Book rate Day 1	AUD	500,000	1.4400	USD	347,222
Book rate Day 2	AUD	500,000	1.4550	USD	343,643
					3,580
(Long base currency and an increase in rate = gains in exchange)					

Net loss in spot exchange position revaluation is USD1,448 (5,028-3,580)

VR16-5	Ccy	Dr	Cr
USD LEDGER : Accounts			
Spot exc revaluation p&l	USD	1,448	
Spot exchange position	USD		1,448

Fig. 28 Asset-Liabilities after revaluation on Day 2 (Gains/loss taken up in book base currency)

	USD Ledger		SGD Ledger		AUD Ledger		Reporting USD	
	Assets	Liabilities	Assets	Liabilities	Assets	Liabilities	Assets	Liabilities
Other Assets-Liabilities	3,000,000	3,000,000	2,000,000	2,000,000	1,000,000	1,000,000	5,147,139	5,147,139
Nostro	0	0	465,000	0	0	500,000	339,416	343,643
Spot exchange position	0	4,226	0	465,000	500,000	0	343,643	343,642
Fwd Exc revaluation	0	0	0	0	0	0	0	0
P&L equity	0	0	0	0	0	0	0	0
Realised Exc p&l	2,778	0	0	0	0	0	2,778	0
Unrealised Exc p&l	0	0	0	0	0	0	0	0
Spot exc revaluation p&l	1,448	0	0	0	0	0	1,448	0
TOTAL	3,004,226	3,004,226	2,465,000	2,465,000	1,500,000	1,500,000	5,834,424	5,834,424
Book rates	1.0000	1.0000	1.3700	1.3700	1.45500	1.45500		
Translated to USD	3,004,226	3,004,226	1,799,270	1,799,270	1,030,928	1,030,928	5,834,424	5,834,424

Spot exchange positions are eliminated. $1 difference is due to rounding errors.

Does it matter in which currency the exchange gains or loss is taken up

Realised exchange loss taken in the currencies on Day 1 is AUD2,000 and SGD1,875 (see Val16-1 above). Converted on Day 1 (AUD2,000/1.4400 =USD1,389 + SGD1,875/1.3500 =USD1, 389) = USD2,778. This is exactly same as when the gain or loss is taken in book base currency USD. (Val16-3 above).

However, the impact on spot exchange position revaluation is different. When booked in cross currencies, the spot position revaluation on Day 2 is US1,483 (Val16-2) but when taken in book base currency the loss is USD1,448 (Val16-4)

There is a difference of USD35 (1,448–1,448). In a business where trades are written in millions of dollars and hundreds of trades are transacted daily, this small difference translates to significant impact on profit and loss.

This difference is explained by :

- Volume difference - Where the realised gains or losses are taken up in the cross currencies, they create spot exchange positions in the relevant currencies. Where the gains or losses are taken up in the book base currency, the spot exchange positions of the cross currencies remain unchanged. The 2 different methods result in different spot exchange positions causing a variance in revaluation gains and losses.
- Rate change difference - The two cross currencies do not move against the book base currency at the same rate. That is, the USD/AUD and USD/SGD rates do not move by the same percentages.

Unrealised exchange gains or losses are different. Because they do not create any spot exchange positions, it matters not in which currency unrealised gains or losses are booked.

Since there is a financial impact, the policy on which currency should take up the gains or losses is thus the Treasurer's decision, and not the Accountant's to make as required by IAS21. What the accountant would insist is the consistency of the policy, once established.

****

17. What is FX Arbitrage

An arbitrage is the simultaneous buying and selling of an asset across different markets in order to take advantage of price differentials. An interconnected world and trading algorithms have made markets m0re perfect, which diminishes arbitrage opportunities. Nevertheless, such opportunities still exist within very narrow window of time, often in seconds. The spreads are very thin. All this means it is possible only at wholesale levels, speedy execution of trades, and use of high technology.

Foreign exchange arbitrage can be in several ways :

- buy spot in one market and selling in another.
- buy futures in one market and sell in another.
- spot-futures arbitrage - buying in the spot and selling in the futures market (basically, an FX swap)
- triangular arbitrage, or cross rates, eg buy USD/YEN, sell EUR/YEN, buy EUR/USD.
- uncovered arbitrage - buy at spot market and invest the currency received at higher interest rate.
- covered interest parity arbitrage - buy at spot, invest currency received, and sell at future date of investment maturity.

The last form of FX arbitrage is known as Covered Interest Parity (CIP) which, as mentioned in chapter 9, theoretically has no arbitrage opportunities as communication and technology advanced to create a perfect market. But as some studies show, such as the BIS (Bank for International Settlement) working papers of 2017 by Dagfinn Rime, Andreas Schrimpf and Olav Syrstad showed, CIP has in fact thrived after 2008. Segmented money markets and the rise of central bank liquidity from massive quantitative easing after the financial crisis of 2008, has provided top tier banks with cheap source of funds to offer. With cost of funds advantage, these top tier banks can act as market makers and offer prices that allow them to fill their order books.

The CIP FX arbitrage:

In a CIP FX arbitrage there are basically 4 transactions,

1. A borrowed fund in the money market.
2. A spot exchange to convert the borrowed fund into another currency
3. Invest the derived fund in the money market
4. A forward exchange to convert the invested funds on maturity to repay the borrowed funds.

The general concept is to borrow a currency with a lower interest rate and then invest it in another currency with a higher interest rate. This will enable some net interest gains. As mentioned previously, given currency equilibrium, the forward spot rate will be the ratio of the borrowed funds + interest and the invested fund + interest. That is the expected exchange rate at the maturity date. The forward rate of exchange in (4) should converge with the expected rate under the interest rate parity principle. Thus there is no arbitrage opportunity.

But when the forward exchange rate does not converge with the expected rate, an arbitrage opportunity exists. It is a question of whether the spread is large enough to cover the costs. A further point to note is that it is not a matter of looking at interest rate differentials, but rather the foreign exchange rates. What this means is that arbitrage transactions may also involve borrowing a currency with a higher interest rate and investing in another currency with a lower rate.

It should be pointed out that the back and middle offices process these external market transactions without being aware they form part of an FX arbitrage strategy. They simply handle them as 4 ordinary FX and money market transactions. As for the Arbitrage tickets, they process these with no reference to underlying market transactions.

****

17.1 Illustration of a CIP FX arbitrage

The front office executed a CIP FX arbitrage strategy and issues the relevant external deal tickets on Jun 8 :

External deal tickets :

1. Spot FX deal #55 sell 5,000,000 GBP/USD at spot 1.2300 value Jun 10
2. Forward FX deal #31 buy 5,017,188 GBP/USD at 1.2306 value Sep 9
3. Money market Acceptance #44 GBP5,000,000 @ 1.3750 % Jun 10 - Sep 9
4. Money market Placement #21 USD6,150,000 @ 1.7500 % Jun 10 - Sep 9

The bank borrows GBP for 3 months, converts it to USD which is invested for 3 months, and arranges a forward FX deal to cover the borrowed funds principal + interest. The profit for this strategy :

Tab17-1-1		Borrowed		Invested
		GBP		USD
Spot FX		5,000,000	1.2300	6,150,000
Interest for 3 months	1.3750%	17,188	1.7500%	26,906
No-arbitrage rate		5,017,188	1.231149	6,176,906
Forward FX		5,017,188	1.2306	6,174,151
Profit				2,755

The **expected rate** in 3 months is 1.231149. If the forward rate converges at the expected rate, there is no arbitrage opportunity. There is arbitrage profit if the rate is anywhere below 1.231149. Since the bank is able to get a deal at 1.2306, there is a profit to be made.

<u>The normal Profit & loss ramifications of the 4 external deals:</u>

1. The GBP books will show a gross interest expense of GBP17,188 without investment returns.
2. The USD books will show a gross interest income of USD26,906 without any cost of funds.
3. Both the spot and forward FX deals will cause open forward exchange positions and subject to forward revaluation for everyday they remain in the contingent accounts.
4. Both the spot and forward FX deals are subject to realised exchange valuation on settlement or value date.
5. On settlement, both the spot and forward FX deals create open spot exchange positions which are then subject to daily revaluation.

There is a net investment return of USD2,755. The bank recognises it as a net interest return. CIP FX Arbitrage deals are handled by the money market desk of banks. The 2 FX deals will throw up exchange gains or losses even though it is a fully covered transaction. So there is a situation of FX revaluation distorting the investment objective. Operationally, it is also a problem of messing up profit centre responsibilities. The FX desk may get hit by positions not opened by them and for which they are not aware of. Accounting intercession is required to overcome this debacle.

The Arbitrage Ticket:

The arbitrage ticket is used to generate some internal transactions that will eliminate exchange positions caused by the 2 FX deals, as well as to switch the funding cost from the borrowed currency to the investing currency. The result of the arbitrage ticket is to show the CIP FX arbitrage as strictly an investment objective with a net interest earning of USD2,755.

No back or middle office personnel can originate any treasury transaction. The arbitrage ticket is issued by the money market desk that wrote the CIP FX arbitrage.

When dealers (front office) talk of arbitrage, they mean the CIP FX arbitrage. When back and middle office talk of arbitrage, they mean these internal arbitrage tickets.

The front office issues arbitrage ticket AB#222 which will generate various nominal transactions – 2 nominal FX transactions on opposite sides of the external FX deals for the spot and forward legs, a notional placement (deposits with) transaction to eliminate the GBP cost of funds, and a nominal acceptance (deposits from) transaction at an engineered rate to apply a USD cost of funds.

The nominal internal transactions:

1. Arbitrage spot FX buy 5,000,000 GBP/USD at 1.2300 value Jun 10
2. Arbitrage forward FX sell 5,017,188 GBP/USD at 1.2306 value Sep 9
3. Arbitrage notional placement GBP5,000,000 at 1.37500% for Jun 10-Sep 9
4. Arbitrage notional acceptance USD6,150,000 is set at **1.5708%** for Jun 10-Sep 9.

How the deals cancel out:

Effects on realised exchange p&l

On Jun 10 commencement of spot leg, the external FX deal's realised exchange gain is canceled out by the nominal arbitrage ticket. (Book rate is assumed. It does not mater which rate is used, the numbers will cancel out.)

Val17-1-1	Ccy	Amount	Rate	Ccy	Amount
FX deal #55					
Contract	GBP	5,000,000	1.2300	USD	500,000
Book rate (Jun 10)	GBP	5,000,000	1.2295	USD	496,000
Gain				USD	4,000

Sell base currency, decrease in rates = gain in exchange

Val17-1-2	Ccy	Amount	Rate	Ccy	Amount
AB #222					
Contract	GBP	5,000,000	1.2300	USD	500,000
Book rate (Jun 10)	GBP	5,000,000	1.2295	USD	496,000
Loss				USD	4,000

Buy base currency, decrease in rates = loss in exchange

Similarly, on Sep 9 value date of forward leg, realised exchange p&l is canceled out thus (once again we assume a book rate)

Val17-1-3	Ccy	Amount	Rate	Ccy	Amount
FX deal #35					
Contract	GBP	5,017,188	1.2306	USD	6,174,152
Book rate (Sep 9)	GBP	5,017,188	1.2311	USD	6,176,660
Loss				USD	-2,509

Sell base currency, increase in rates = loss in exchange

Val17-1-4	Ccy	Amount	Rate	Ccy	Amount
AB #222					
Contract	GBP	5,017,188	1.2306	USD	6,174,152
Book rate (Sep 9)	GBP	5,017,188	1.2311	USD	6,176,660
Gain				USD	-2,509

Buy base currency, increase in rates = loss in exchange

Effects on unrealised exchange p&l:

From deal inception date of Jun 8 to value dates Jun 10 and Sep 9, both the external FX deals and the nominal deals generated by the arbitrage ticket are subject to forward revaluation daily. Just as for realised exchange p&l, they have no impact on unrealised exchange p&l. They cancel each other out.

Effects on spot exchange revaluation:

The cashflows generated by the external deals on settlement dates create spot exchange positions. However these positions are eliminated by the reverse nominal positions created by the arbitrage ticket. There is thus no spot exchange revaluation.

Effects on interest revenue/expenses:

The money market acceptance or borrowed funds of GBP5,000,000 and the nominal deposits of arbitrage ticket AB#222 are both priced at 1.3750% p.a .They thus cancel each other out in the GBP ledger.

The way the whole scheme works rests on how the price of the notional deposit generated by arbitrage ticket AB #222 is computed. This in an engineered computation to work out a cost-of-funds that will produce an interest of USD24,151 so as to derive at net investment earnings of USD2,755. The interest rate for the notional arbitrage acceptance is 1.5708% p.a.

Tab17-1-2	USD
Money Market placement USD6,150,000 x 1.75% x 3 months	26,906
Arbitrage acceptance USD6,150,000 x 1.5708% x 3 months	24,151
Net interest income	2,755

If you think it is a very contrived process, wait till you see the work cut out for the middle office. Considering there is no big money to be made in a CIP arbitrage, thanks to a perfect market brought about by instantaneous communication, and considering too the vast sums of money moved around and tremendous processing power required of the middle office, the issue of cost effectiveness remains. The USD2,755 is not pure profit. There are other costs such as settlement and risks associated costs.

Fortunately, computerisation has relieved middle office of attendant mundane processing work On the other hand, automation has distanced bank employees from the kind of deep knowledge one gains from the trenches. The average lower level staff members in a bank today are unlikely to appreciate what goes on in accounting behind a CIP arbitrage.

****

17.2 Accounting entries for FX arbitrage

These are the accounting entries for the illustrated CIP FX arbitrage, together with the entries for the arbitrage ticket. If it looks like there is a lot of work involved, indeed it does. In fact, the daily interest accruals and forward exchange revaluation have been omitted in the illustration to avoid clutter. Only the final interest postings are shown here.

The author has seen the incredibly laborious month end computation of interest accruals and amortisation of arbitrage offsets by the back and middle office during pre-spreadsheet and computer days. Today, these functions are fully automated

(A) Jun 8 – Deal inception of spot leg of the CIP arbitrage (FX deal # 55) value Jun 10

VR17-2-1	Ccy	Dr	Cr
USD LEDGER Accounts			
FX purchased	USD	6,150,000	
Forward exc position GBP/USD	USD		6,150,000
GBP LEDGER Accounts			
Forward exc position GBP/USD	GBP	5,000,000	
FX sold	GBP		5,000,000

(B) Jun 8 – Deal inception of spot leg of the nominal FX from Arbitrage ticket AB#222) Value Jun 10

VR17-2-2	Ccy	Dr	Cr
USD LEDGER Accounts			
Forward exc position GBP/USD	USD	6,150,000	
FX sold	USD		6,150,000
GBP LEDGER Accounts			
FX purchased	GBP	5,000,000	
Forward exc position GBP/USD	GBP		5,000,000

(C) Jun 8 – Deal inception of forward leg of the CIP Arbitrage (FX deal #31) Value Sep 9

VR17-2-3	Ccy	Dr	Cr
USD LEDGER Accounts			
Forward exc position GBP/USD	USD	6,174,151	
FX sold	USD		6,174,151
GBP LEDGER Accounts			
FX purchased	GBP	5,017,188	
Forward exc position GBP/USD	GBP		5,017,188

(D) Jun 8 – Deal inception of forward leg of the nominal FX from Arbitrage Ticket AB #222 Value Sep 9

VR17-2-4	Ccy	Dr	Cr
USD LEDGER Accounts			
FX purchased	USD	6,174,151	
Forward exc position GBP/USD	USD		6,174,151
GBP LEDGER Accounts			
Forward exc position GBP/USD	GBP	5,017,188	
FX sold	GBP		5,017,188

(E) Jun 10 – Deal settlement of spot leg of CIP Arbitrage (FX deal #55)

VR17-2-5	Ccy	Dr	Cr
USD LEDGER Accounts			
Forward exch position GBP/USD	USD	6,150,000	
FX purchased	USD		6,150,000
Nostro	USD	6,150,000	
Spot exchange position	USD		6,150,000
GBP LEDGER Accounts	Ccy		
FX sold	GBP	5,000,000	
Forward exc position GBP/USD	GBP		5,000,000
Spot exchange position	GBP	5,000,000	
Nostro	GBP		5,000,000

(F) Jun 10 – Deal settlement of spot leg of nominal FX of Arbitrage Ticket AB#222

VR17-2-6	Ccy	Dr	Cr
USD LEDGER Accounts			
FX sold	USD	6,150,000	
Forward exc position GBP/USD	USD		6,150,000
Spot exchange position	USD	6,150,000	
Arbitrage suspense	USD		6,150,000
GBP LEDGER Accounts			
Forward exc position GBP/USD	GBP	5,000,000	
FX purchased	GBP		5,000,000
Arbitrage suspense	GBP	5,000,000	
Spot exchange position	GBP		5,000,000

(G) Jun 10 realised exchange p&l of FX deal #55

VR17-2-7	Ccy	Dr	Cr
USD LEDGER : Accounts			
Spot exchange position	USD	1,000	
Realised Exchange p&l	USD		1,000

(H) Jun 10 realised exchange p&l of nominal FX from arbitrage ticket AB #222

VR17-2-8	Ccy	Dr	Cr
USD LEDGER : Accounts			
Realised Exchange p&l	USD	1,000	
Spot exchange position	USD		1,000

(I) Jun 10 – Deal inception of Borrowed funds (MM Acceptance # 44)

VR17-2-9	Ccy	Dr	Cr
GBP LEDGER Accounts			
Nostro	GBP	5,000,000	
Deposits from banks	GBP		5,000,000

(J) Jun 10 – Deal inception of Invested funds (MM Placement # 21)

VR17-2-10	Ccy	Dr	Cr
USD LEDGER Accounts			
Deposits with banks	USD	6,150,000	
Nostro	USD		6,150,000

(K) Jun 10 - Sep 9 Interest accruals on money market Placements #21 and Acceptances #44.
Note: This is done daily, but for illustration here, let's just lump the daily entries together on Sep 9

VR17-2-11	Ccy	Dr	Cr
USD LEDGER Accounts			
Interest receivable	USD	26,906	
Interest revenue	USD		26,906
GBP LEDGER Accounts			
Interest expense	GBP	17,188	
Interest payable	GBP		17,188

(L) Jun 10 - Sep 9 Nominal interest accruals on arbitrage ticket AB #222
Note: This is done daily, but for illustration here, let's just lump the daily entries together on Sep 9.

VR17-2-12	Ccy	Dr	Cr
USD LEDGER Accounts			
Interest expense	USD	24,151	
Interest payable	USD		24,151
GBP LEDGER Accounts			
Interest receivable	GBP	17,188	
Interest revenue	GBP		17,188

(M) Sep 9 Repayment of borrowed funds principal + interest (MM Acceptance # 44) on maturity date

VR17-2-13	Ccy	Dr	Cr
GBP LEDGER Accounts			
Deposit from banks	GBP	5,000,000	
Interest payable	GBP	17,188	
Nostro	GBP		5,017,188

(N) Sep 9 Withdrawal of invested funds principal + interest (MM Placement # 21) on maturity date

VR17-2-14	Ccy	Dr	Cr
USD LEDGER Accounts			
Nostro	USD	6,176,906	
Deposits with banks	USD		6,150,000
Interest receivable	USD		26,906

(O) Sep 9 – Deal maturity settlement of forward leg of CIP Arbitrage (FX deal #31)

VR17-2-15	Ccy	Dr	Cr
USD LEDGER Accounts			
FX sold	USD	6,174,151	
Forward exc position GBP/USD	USD		6,174,151
Spot exchange position	USD	6,174,151	
Nostro	USD		6,174,151,
GBP LEDGER Accounts			
Forward exc position GBP/USD	GBP	5,017,188	
FX purchased	GBP		5,017,188
Nostro	GBP	5,017,188	
Spot exchange position	GBP		5,017,188

(P) Sep 9 Deal maturity of forward leg of nominal FX from Arbitrage Ticket AB#222

VR17-2-16	Ccy	Dr	Cr
USD LEDGER Accounts			
Forward exc position GBP/USD	USD	6,174,151	
FX purchased	USD		6,174,151
Interest payable	USD	24,151	
Arbitrage suspense	USD	6,150,000	
Spot exchange position			6,174,151
GBP LEDGER Accounts			
FX sold	GBP	5,017,188	
Forward exc position GBP/USD	GBP		5,017,188
Spot exchange position	GBP	5,017,188	
Arbitrage suspense	GBP		5,000,000
Interest receivable	GBP		17,188

(Q) Sep 9 realised exchange p&l of FX deal #55

VR17-2-17	Ccy	Dr	Cr
USD LEDGER : Accounts			
Realised Exchange p&l	USD	2,509	
Spot exchange position	USD		2,509

(R) Sep 9 realised exchange p&l of nominal FX from arbitrage ticket AB #222

VR17-2-18	Ccy	Dr	Cr
USD LEDGER : Accounts			
Spot exchange position	USD	2,509	
Realised Exchange p&l	USD		2,509

NOTE

Daily interest accruals are not shown here. Only the final interest revenue and expense entries are shown.

Daily forward unrealised exchange gains or losses on the external FX deals and nominal FX from arbitrage ticket AB #222 are also not shown. These cancel each other our effectively.

****

17.3 USD Ledger

AC17-3-1		A/c : FX purchased	Dr	Cr	Balance
Date	Ref	Details	USD	USD	USD
Jun 8	D	Arbitrage Fwd FX	-6,174,151		-12,324,151
Jun 10	E	Settlement - Spot FX#55		6,150,000	-6,174,151
Sep 9	P	Arbitrage Fwd FX maturity		6,174,151	0

AC17-3-2		Account : FX sold	Dr	Cr	Balance
Date	Ref	Details	USD	USD	USD
Jun 8	B	Arbitrage spot FX		6,150,000	6,150,000
Jun 8	C	Inception - Fwd FX #31		6,174,151	12,324,151
Jun 10	F	Arbitrage spot FX maturity	-6,150,000		6,174,151
Sep 9	O	Settlement Fwd FX#31	-6,174,151		0

AC17-3-3		A/c : Fwd exc position GBP/USD	Dr	Cr	Balance
Date	Ref	Details	USD	USD	USD
Jun 8	A	Inception -Spot FX #55		6,150,000	6,150,000
Jun 8	B	Arbitrage spot FX	-6,150,000		0
Jun 8	C	Inception - Fwd FX #31	-6,174,151		-6,174,151
Jun 8	D	Arbitrage fwd FX		6,174,151	0
Jun 10	E	Settlement - spot FX #55	-6,150,000		-6,150,000
Jun 10	F	Arbitrage spot FX maturity		6,150,000	0
Sep 9	O	Settlement - Fwd FX #31		6,174,151	6,174,151
Sep 9	P	Arbitrage fwd FX maturity	-6,174,151		0

AC17-3-4		A/c : Spot exchange position	Dr	Cr	Balance
Date	Ref	Details	USD	USD	USD
Jun 10	E	Settlement - spot FX #55		6,150,000	6,150,000
Jun 10	F	Arbitrage spot FX maturity	-6,150,000		0
Jun 10	G	Realised exchange gains FX #55	-1,000		-1,000
Jun 10	H	Realised exchange loss AB #222		1,000	0
Sep 9	O	Settlement - Fwd FX #31	-6,174,151		-6,174,151
Sep 9	P	Arbitrage tkt #222 maturity		6,174,151	0
Sep 9	Q	Realised exchange loss FX #31		2,509	2,509
Sep 9	R	Realised exchange gains AB #222	-2,509		0

AC17-3-5		A/c : Arbitrage suspense	Dr	Cr	Balance
Date	Ref	Details	USD	USD	USD
Jun 10	F	Arbitrage spot FX maturity		6,150,000	6,150,000
Sep 9	P	Arbitrage tkt #222 maturity	-6,150,000		0

AC17-3-6		A/c : Nostro	Dr	Cr	Balance
6	Ref	Details	USD	USD	USD
Jun 10	E	Settlement - spot FX #55	-6,150,000		-6,150,000
Jun 10	I	MM placement #44		6,150,000	0
Sep 9	N	MM placement #44 maturity	-6,176,906		-6,176,906
Sep 9	O	Settlement - Fwd FX #31		6,174,151	-2,755

AC17-3-7		A/c : Deposits with banks	Dr	Cr	Balance
Date	Ref	Details	USD	USD	USD
Jun 10	J	MM placement #44	-6,150,000		-6,150,000
Sep 9	N	MM placement #44 maturity		6,150,000	0

AC17-3-8		A/c : Interest receivable	Dr	Cr	Balance
Date	Ref	Details	USD	USD	USD
Sep 9	K	MM placement #44	-26,906		-26,906
Sep 9	N	MM placement #44 maturity		26,906	0

AC17-3-9		A/c : Interest payable	Dr	Cr	Balance
Date	Ref	Details	USD	USD	USD
Sep 9	L	Arbitrage ticket #222		24,151	24,151
Sep 9	O	Arbitrage tkt #222 maturity	-24,151		0

AC17-3-10		A/c : Interest revenue	Dr	Cr	Balance
Date	Ref	Details	USD	USD	USD
Sep 9	K	MM placement #44		26,906	26,906

AC17-3-11		A/c : Interest expense	Dr	Cr	Balance
Date	Ref	Details	USD	USD	USD
Sep 9	L	Arbitrage ticket #222	24,151		-24,151

AC17-3-12		A/c : Realised exchange p&l	Dr	Cr	Balance
Date	Ref	Details	USD	USD	USD
Jun 10	G	Realised exchange gains FX #55		1,000	1,000
Jun 10	H	Realised exchange loss AB #222	-1,000		0
Sep 9	Q	Realised exchange loss FX #31	-2,509		-2,509
Sep 9	R	Realised exchange gains AB #222		2,509	0

****

17.4 GBP Ledger

AC17-4-1		A/c : FX purchased	Dr	Cr	Balance
Date	Ref	Details	GBP	GBP	GBP
Jun 8	B	Arbitrage spot FX	-5,000,000		-5,000,000
Jun 8	C	Inception - Fwd FX #31	-5,017,188		-10,017,188
Jun10	F	Arbitrage spot FX maturity		5,000,000	-5,017,188
Sep 9	O	Settlement - Fwd FX #31		5,017,188	0

AC17-4-2		A/c : FX sold	Dr	Cr	Balance
Date	Ref	Details	GBP	GBP	GBP
Jun 8	A	Inception - Spot FX #55		5,000,000	5,000,000
Jun 8	D	Arbitrage Fwd FX		5,017,188	10,017,188
Jun10	E	Settlement - Spot FX #55	-5,000,000		5,017,188
Sep 9	P	Arbitrage Fwd FX maturity	-5,017,188		0

AC17-4-3		A/c : Fwd exc position GBP/USD	Dr	Cr	Balance
Date	Ref	Details	GBP	GBP	GBP
Jun 8	A	Incepton - Spot FX #55	-5,000,000		5,000,000
Jun 8	B	Arbitrage spot FX		5,000,000	0
Jun 8	C	Inception - Fwd FX #31		5,017,188	5,017,188
Jun 8	D	Arbitrage fwd FX	-5,017,188		0
Jun10	E	Settlement - Spot FX #55		5,000,000	-5,000,000
Jun10	F	Arbitrage spot FX maturity	-5,000,000		0
Sep 9	O	Settlement - Fwd FX #31	-5,017,188		5,017,188
Sep 9	P	Fwd arbitrage FX maturity		5,017,188	0

AC17-4-4		A/c : Spot exchange position	Dr	Cr	Balance
Date	Ref	Details	GBP	GBP	GBP
Jun10	E	Settlement - Spot FX #55	-5,000,000		-5,000,000
Jun10	F	Arbitrage spot FX maturity		5,000,000	0
Sep 9	O	Settlement - Fwd FX #31		5,017,188	5,017,188
Sep 9	P	Arbitrage fwd FX maturity	-5,017,188		0

AC17-4-5		A/c : Arbitrage suspense	Dr	Cr	Balance
Date	Ref	Details	GBP	GBP	GBP
Jun10	F	Arbitrage spot FX maturity	-5,000,000		-5,000,000
Sep 9	P	Arbitrage fwd FX maturity		5,000,000	0

AC17-4-6		A/c : Nostro	Dr	Cr	Balance
Date	Ref	Details	GBP	GBP	GBP
Jun10	E	Settlement - spot FX #55		5,000,000	5,000,000
Jun10	I	MM acceptance #011	-5,000,000		0
Sep 9	L	MM acceptce #011 maturity		5,017,188	5,017,188
Sep 9	O	Settlement - Fwd FX #31	-5,017,188		0

AC17-4-7		A/c : Deposits from banks	Dr	Cr	Balance
Date	Ref	Details	GBP	GBP	GBP
Jun10	I	MM acceptance #21		5,000,000	5,000,000
Sep 9	M	MM acceptance #21 maturity	-5,000,000		0

AC17-4-8		A/c : Interest receivable	Dr	Cr	Balance
Date	Ref	Details	GBP	GBP	GBP
Sep 9	L	Arbitrage ticket #222	-17,188		-17,188
Sep 9	P	Arbitrage tkt #222 maturity		17,188	0

AC17-4-9		A/c :Interest payable	Dr	Cr	Balance
Date	Ref	Details	GBP	GBP	GBP
Sep 9	K	MM acceptance #21		17,188	17,188
Sep 9	M	MM acceptance #21 maturity	-17,188		0

AC17-4-10		A/c :Interest revenue	Dr	Cr	Balance
Date	Ref	Details	GBP	GBP	GBP
Sep 9	L	Arbitrage ticket #222		17,188	17,188

AC17-4-11		A/c :Interest expense	Dr	Cr	Balance
Date	Ref	Details	GBP	GBP	GBP
Sep 9	K	MM acceptance #21	-17,188		-17,188

****

17.5 Asset-Liability view of arbitrage

The asset-liability view clearly shows the accounting intercession of the internal arbitrage ticket has the effects of :

- Closing out the spot and open positions created by the external spot and forward FX deals, thereby neutralising the effect of foreign exchange revaluation on a covered FX arbitrage
- Showing the overall trading result of net interest income in the investing currency, ie USD2,755. The net cash inflow is seen in the balance in the nostro account.

The following tables show the assets-liabilities status on 3 dates :

<u>On deal inception</u>

Fig.29 Assets-Liabilities as at Jun 8 (FX deal inception)

	USD Ledger		GBP Ledger		SGD Ledger	
	Assets	Liabilities	Assets	Liabilities	Assets	Liabilities
OFF BALANCE SHEET						
FX Purchased	12,324,151	0	0	10,017,188	0	0
FX Sold	0	12,324,151	10,017,188	0	0	0
Fwd FX Position GBP/USD	0	0	0	0	0	0
TOTAL	12,324,151	12,324,151	10,017,188	10,017,188	0	0

On spot leg maturity

Fig.30 Assets-Liabilities as at Jun 10 (spot leg maturity)

	USD Ledger		GBP Ledger		SGD Ledger		Reporting USD	
	Assets	Liabilities	Assets	Liabilities	Assets	Liabilities	Assets	Liabilities
Deposits with/from banks	6,150,000	0	0	5,000,000	0	0	6,150,000	6,495,000
Nostro	0	0	0	0	0	0	0	0
Spot exc position	0	0	0	0	0	0	0	0
Fwd exc revaluation	0	0	0	0	0	0	0	0
Arbitrage suspense	0	6,150,000	5,000,000	0	0	0	6,495,000	6,150,000
Interest revenue	0	0	0	0	0	0	0	0
Interest expense	0	0	0	0	0	0	0	0
Realised exc p&l	0	0	0	0	0	0	0	0
Unrealised Exc p&l	0	0	0	0	0	0	0	0
Spot exc revaluation p&l	0	0	0	0	0	0	0	0
TOTAL	6,150,000	6,150,000	5,000,000	5,000,000	0	0	12,645,000	12,645,000
Book rates	1.0000	1.0000	1.2990	1.2990	1.35000	1.35000		
Translated to USD	6,150,000	6,150,000	6,495,000	6,495,000	0	0	12,645,000	12,645,000
OFF BALANCE SHEET								
FX Purchased	6,174,151	0	0	5,017,188	0	0		
FX Sold	0	6,174,151	5,017,188	0	0	0		
Fwd FX Position GBP/USD	0	0	0	0	0	0		
TOTAL	6,174,151	6,174,151	5,017,188	5,017,188	0	0		

On the end date

Fig.31 Assets-Liabilities as at Sep 9 (forward leg maturity)

	USD Ledger		GBP Ledger		SGD Ledger		Reporting USD	
	Assets	Liabilities	Assets	Liabilities	Assets	Liabilities	Assets	Liabilities
Deposits with/from banks	0	0	0	0	0	0	0	0
Nostro	2,755	0	0	0	0	0	2,755	0
Spot exc position	0	0	0	0	0	0	0	0
Fwd exc revaluation	0	0	0	0	0	0	0	0
Arbitrage suspense	0	0	0	0	0	0	0	0
Interest revenue	0	26,906	0	17,188	0	0	0	48,064
Interest expense	24,151	0	17,188	0	0	0	45,309	0
Realised exc p&l	0	0	0	0	0	0	0	0
Unrealised Exc p&l	0	0	0	0	0	0	0	0
Spot exc revaluation p&l	0	0	0	0	0	0	0	0
TOTAL	26,906	26,906	17,188	17,188	0	0	48,064	48,064
Book rates	1.0000	1.0000	1.2310	1.2310	1.35000	1.35000		
Translated to USD	26,906	26,906	21,158	21,158	0	0	48,064	48,064
OFF BALANCE SHEET								
FX Purchased	0	0	0	0	0	0		
FX Sold	0	0	0	0	0	0		
Fwd FX Position GBP/USD	0	0	0	0	0	0		
TOTAL	0	0	0	0	0	0		

Point to note : There are no spot or forward exchange positions. The use of the arbitrage ticket neutralises the exchange positions and reflects the whole operation as a single interest earning transaction.

****

17.6 Risk profiles in a CIP FX arbitrage

The previous chapters show the utility of the arbitrage ticket in switching exchange profit & loss as well as interest revenue and expense to reflect the correct net interest gain in a CIP arbitrage strategy thus preventing distortions to its financial reporting.

The arbitrage ticket actually does more than this.

The 4 external deals, ie the 2 FX deals together with the money market acceptance and placement deals, create risk profiles that should not be there since they form a covered FX arbitrage. The arbitrage ticket is the mechanism to cancel out these risks.

The following demonstrates how the external deals in the illustration create risk profiles which are negated by the arbitrage ticket. For interest rate and maturity ladders, only USD are shown. Similar constructs are available for GBP. The deals in illustration 17-2 are first shown in isolation in risk profile reports without arbitrage tickets. They are then compared to the same risk profiles but with arbitrage tickets included.

Risk profiles without the arbitrage ticket:

Interest rate ladder

This profiles the bank's exposure to changes in interest rate movements. This is a report on interest rate gap sensitivities by individual currencies. All interest-bearing assets and liabilities are aggregated here. The bands (columns) are based on days left to maturity. The maturity is in terms of the interest period, not the final maturity of asset or liability. Eg a 10 year USD1m loan priced at 6 month floating rates is reported according to days to maturity of is current coupon.

Fig 32 Interest rate ladder (no arbitrage) – USD

As at Jun 10									
Currency : USD	Cash	Spot	7 days	1 month	3 months	6 months	12 mths	> 12 mths	Total
Others	0	0	0	0	0	0	0	0	0
Cash / nostros	0	0	0	0	0	0	0	0	0
Reverse repos	0	0	0	0	0	0	0	0	0
Money market	0	0	0	0	-6,150,000	0	0	0	-6,150,000
Securities	0	0	0	0	0	0	0	0	0
Trade finance	0	0	0	0	0	0	0	0	0
Loans	0	0	0	0	0	-1,000,000	0	0	-1,000,000
Arbitrage	0	0	0	0	0	0	0	0	0
Total assets:	0	0	0	0	-6,150,000	-1,000,000	0	0	-7,150,000
Others	0	0	0	0	0	0	0	0	0
Vostros	0	0	0	0	0	0	0	0	0
Customer deposits	0	0	0	0	0	0	0	0	0
Repos	0	0	0	0	0	0	0	0	0
Money market	0	0	0	0	0	0	0	0	0
Bonds issued	0	0	0	0	0	0	0	0	0
Arbitrage	0	0	0	0	0	0	0	0	0
Total liabilities	0	0	0	0	0	0	0	0	0
NET(-) Long (+) Short	0	0	0	0	-6,150,000	-1,000,000	0	0	-7,150,000

Liquidity ladder

This profiles the bank's exposure to liquidity. It shows the open positions of the currency reported. The bands (columns) are based on days left to maturity. The differences of this gaping report is liquidity (1) includes all non-interest bearing assets and liabilities; (2) the maturity here is the final maturity date of the assets or liabilities. The 10 year loan is reported in the 12 months column in the liquidity ladder report.

Fig.33 Liquidity ladder (no arbitrage) - USD

As at Jun 10									
Currency : USD	Cash	Spot	7 days	1 month	3 months	6 months	12 mths	> 12 mths	Total
Others	0	0	0	0	0	0	0	0	0
Cash / nostros	0	0	0	0	0	0	0	0	0
Reverse repos	0	0	0	0	0	0	0	0	0
Money market	0	0	0	0	-6,150,000	0	0	0	-6,150,000
Securities	0	0	0	0	0	0	0	0	0
Trade finance	0	0	0	0	0	0	0	0	0
Loans	0	0	0	0	0	0	0	-1,000,000	-1,000,000
Arbitrage	0	0	0	0	0	0	0	0	0
Total assets:	0	0	0	0	-6,150,000	0	0	-1,000,000	-7,150,000
Others	0	0	0	0	0	0	0	0	0
Vostros	0	0	0	0	0	0	0	0	0
Customer deposits	0	0	0	0	0	0	0	0	0
Repos	0	0	0	0	0	0	0	0	0
Money market	0	0	0	0	0	0	0	0	0
Bonds issued	0	0	0	0	0	0	0	0	0
Arbitrage	0	0	0	0	0	0	0	0	0
Total liabilities	0	0	0	0	0	0	0	0	0
NET(-) Long (+) Short	0	0	0	0	6,150,000	0	0	-1,000,000	-7,150,000

Trading positions

This profiles the bank's exposure to changes in exchange rates. It shows the carry positions by currency pairs. The bands (columns) are based on days left to maturity.

Fig.34 Trading position (no arbitrage) - GBP/USD

As at Jun 10								
Currencies : GBP/USD	Spot	7 days	1 month	3 months	6 months	12 months	> 12 mths	Total
FX Buy	0	0	0	-5,000,000	0	0	0	-5,000,000
FX Sell	0	0	0	0	0	0	0	0
NET (-) Long (+) Short	0	0	0	-5,000,000	0	0	0	-5,000,000

Risk profiles with the arbitrage ticket

The arbitrage ticket eliminates all the positions created by the 4 external deals in the CIP arbitrage strategy.

Interest rate ladder

Fig.35 Interest rate ladder (with arbitrage) USD

As at Jun 10									
Currency : USD	Cash	Spot	7 days	1 month	3 months	6 months	12 mths	> 12 mths	Total
Others	0	0	0	0	0	0	0	0	0
Cash / nostros	0	0	0	0	0	0	0	0	0
Reverse repos	0	0	0	0	0	0	0	0	0
Money market	0	0	0	0	-6,150,000	0	0	0	-6,150,000
Securities	0	0	0	0	0	0	0	0	0
Trade finance	0	0	0	0	0	0	0	0	0
Loans	0	0	0	0	0	-1,000,000	0	0	-1,000,000
Arbitrage	0	0	0	0	0	0	0	0	0
Total assets:	0	0	0	0	-6,150,000	-1,000,000	0	0	-7,150,000
Others	0	0	0	0	0	0	0	0	0
Vostros	0	0	0	0	0	0	0	0	0
Customer deposits	0	0	0	0	0	0	0	0	0
Repos	0	0	0	0	0	0	0	0	0
Money market	0	0	0	0	0	0	0	0	0
Bonds issued	0	0	0	0	0	0	0	0	0
Arbitrage	0	0	0	0	6,150,000	0	0	0	6,150,000
Total liabilities	0	0	0	0	6,150,000	0	0	0	6,150,000
NET(-) Long (+) Short	0	0	0	0	0	-1,000,000	0	0	-1,000,000

Liquidity ladder

Fig.36 Liquidity ladder (with arbitrage) USD

As at Jun 10									
Currency : USD	Cash	Spot	7 days	1 month	3 months	6 months	12 mths	> 12 mths	Total
Others	0	0	0	0	0	0	0	0	0
Cash / nostros	0	0	0	0	0	0	0	0	0
Reverse repos	0	0	0	0	0	0	0	0	0
Money market	0	0	0	0	-6,150,000	0	0	0	-6,150,000
Securities	0	0	0	0	0	0	0	0	0
Trade finance	0	0	0	0	0	0	0	0	0
Loans	0	0	0	0	0	0	0	-1,000,000	-1,000,000
Arbitrage	0	0	0	0	0	0	0	0	0
Total assets:	0	0	0	0	-6,150,000	0		-1,000,000	-7,150,000
Others	0	0	0	0	0	0	0	0	0
Vostros	0	0	0	0	0	0	0	0	0
Customer deposits	0	0	0	0	0	0	0	0	0
Repos	0	0	0	0	0	0	0	0	0
Money market	0	0	0	0	0	0	0	0	0
Bonds issued	0	0	0	0	0	0	0	0	0
Arbitrage	0	0	0	0	6,150,000	0	0	0	6,150,000
Total liabilities	0	0	0	0	6,150,000	0	0	0	6,150,000
NET(-) Long (+) Short	0	0	0	0	0	0	0	-1,000,000	-1,000,000

Trading position

Fig.37 Trading position (with arbitrage) – GBP/USD

As at Jun 10								
Currencies : GBP/USD	Spot	7 days	1 month	3 months	6 months	12 months	> 12 mths	Total
FX Buy	0	0	0	-5,000,000	0	0	0	-5,000,000
FX Sell	0	0	0	0	0	0	0	0
Sub-total	0	0	0	-5,000,000	0	0	0	-5,000,000
Arbitrage Buy	0	0	0	0	0	0	0	0
Arbitrage Sell	0	0	0	5,000,000	0	0	0	5,000,000
Sub-total		0	0	5,000,000	0	0	0	5,000,000
NET(-) Long (+) Short	0	0	0	0	0	0	0	0

****

18. Presentation of revenue & expense statements

(A) In single currency accounting systems:

Transactions are recognised and recorded in the functional currency based on historical rates, i.e., the rates on the date of transaction. For year end financial statements they are translated to the presentation or reporting currency at year end rates.

A company having overseas operations may have to deal with foreign branches, subsidiaries, joint ventures that report in different currencies. To consolidate into its accounts, the revenue and expense accounts are translated based on average monthly rates.

Take an example of a US company working on its Australian branch financials.

Financial reports are prepared by converting monthly foreign currency p&l to the book base average rate of each month. The difference is charged off to exchange gains or loss and taken into a reserve account.

Tab18-1				
				Presentation
Month	Ledger	Rate		currency
	AUD	Month end	Average	USD
1	240,000	1.2000	1.1700	205,128
2	270,500	1.2050	1.1750	230,213
3	420,500	1.2150	1.1880	353,956
4	470,445	1.2450	1.2380	380,004
5	455,000	1.2500	1.2485	364,437
6	505,000	1.3000	1.2700	397,638
7	560,220	1.3800	1.3680	409,518
8	540,200	1.4200	1.3885	389,053
9	500,700	1.4250	1.4225	351,986
10	560,705	1.4400	1.4377	390,001
11	460,700	1.4700	1.4600	315,548
12	470,800	1.5000	1.4850	317,037
Total	5,454,770			4,104,519
	1.5000			
	3,636,513			

Foreign entity profit of AUD5,454,770 @ year end rate of .1.500 = USD3,636,513. Translating at monthly average rate results in profit of USD4,104,59. There is a difference of USD468,006 (4,104,519-3,636,513) to be adjusted for gains in exchange on translation.

- Credit Profit & Loss A/C
- Debit Reserves A/C

(B) In multi-currency accounting systems:

Revenue and expense transactions are recognised and recorded in the actual currency ledger. Conversion at historical rates to base currency does not apply. The revenue and expense accounts for each currency ledger are closed off to the respective currency equity Profit & Loss A/c at the end of each accounting period, normally monthly. The currency monthly profit & loss data are available for statement requests any time retrospectively.

A currency consolidated profit and loss statement for any reporting period can be generated in any presentation currency. Consolidated p&l statement is based on individual currency p&l data translated to reporting currency based on book rates at the reporting period end date.

Suppose this same AUD figures are from bank's AUD currency ledger:

Tab18-2	P&L REPORTING IN MULTI-CURRENCY SYSTEM				
	MONTHLY			MONTH-TO-DATE	
	Ledger AUD	Rate Month end	Reporting ccy USD	Ledger AUD	Reporting ccy USD
1	240,000	1.2000	200,000	240,000	200,000
2	270,500	1.2050	224,481	510,500	423,651
3	420,500	1.2150	346,091	931,000	766,255
4	470,445	1.2450	377,867	1,401,445	1,125,659
5	455,000	1.2500	364,000	1,856,445	1,485,156
6	505,000	1.3000	388,462	2,361,445	1,816,496
7	560,220	1.3800	405,957	2,921,665	2,117,149
8	540,200	1.4200	380,423	3,461,865	2,437,933
9	500,700	1.4250	351,368	3,962,565	2,780,747
10	560,705	1.4400	389,378	4,523,270	3,141,160
11	460,700	1.4700	313,401	4,983,970	3,390,456
12	470,800	1.5000	313,867	5,454,770	3,636,513
Total	5,454,770		4,055,295		
	1.5000				
USD	3,636,513		(1)	(2)	(3)

(1) AUD balances translated at month end rate.
(2) Cumulative month-to-date
(3) Month-to-date AUD translated at each month end rate.

In multi-currency accounting, there is no conversion of revenue and expense accounts to book base currency. All accounts are closed off in respective currency ledgers.

Reporting in any presentation currency is done by consolidating the individual currency cumulative balances translated at the rate of the accounting period end date.

There is an argument to be made that the individual currency Profit and Loss Account which, as composite part of currency assets-liabilities mismatch, represented by the spot exchange position accounts, have already been subject to daily revaluation.

****

19. Recap of accounting standards for FX transactions in banks

1. Accounting standards for handling foreign currency transactions in legacy single currency systems do not address the needs of multi-currency systems used by banks. There is no such thing as 'foreign currencies' in a multi-currency system.

2. Banks use multi-currency accounting systems. A self-balancing ledger is maintained for each currency banks deal in. All revenue, expenses, assets or liabilities are recognised and recorded in the respective currency ledgers. There is no base currency to convert to. Each currency ledger has its own Profit & Loss and Assets & Liabilities accountability. In such systems, the legacy meaning of foreign currency does not apply. Consolidated operational and financial reports in any currency using spot rates at reporting period end date are possible without translation discrepancies as long as there is a daily revaluation of spot exchange positions.

3. In a multi-currency system, a transaction that involves only one currency causes compensating movements in the assets and liabilities in the ledger of the relevant currency. The event does not create an exchange position. Thus, the acquisition or disposal of foreign assets per se has no exchange gains or losses involved. IAS21 requires monetary foreign currency assets or liabilities to be booked at historical rates and revalued at disposal date to compute realised exchange gains or losses. The standard does not address accounting treatment in multi-currency systems.

4. A forward foreign exchange deal whose value date has not arrived is marked-to-market daily by comparing the contracted rate with the expected market rate. The expected rate is computed from the average of reference banks' bid-offered spot rates and interest rate parity model. Forward exchange gains or losses are taken into profit & loss. Revaluation of forward exchange deals is in accordance with the fair value concept of IAS21.

5. Realised foreign exchange gains or losses on FX deals that matured are computed by comparing the contract rate with market spot rates on the date of maturity. This is in accordance with IAS21.

6. In multi-currency systems, all revenue, expenses, assets and liabilities are recorded in the respective currency ledgers. For financial reporting, currency ledgers are consolidated in the reporting currency using the book rates on the reporting date.

7. In multi-currency system, each currency ledger has its respective Profit & Loss a/c Month end closures of revenue and expense accounts are within the respective currency ledger. A consolidated P&L statement extracts the month-to date data (or whatever period) in each currency ledger and translates at the exchange rate as at accounting period end date.

8. The currency asset-liability mismatch is the banks' open spot exchange position in the relevant currencies. As the daily spot rate changes, the value of these open position changes. Banks revalue these open spot positions daily and gains or losses are taken into Profit & Loss. The revaluation of spot positions is in reality the translation of foreign currencies as required by IAS21 but done on a net basis. It is however done daily and not using exchange rates as at the reporting date in accordance with accounting standards.

9. In the case of foreign exchange contracts, they are unique in that the exchange gains or losses can be viewed in terms of either the sell or the buy currency. In the context of multi-currency systems, whichever currency is used to book the gains or losses creates a spot exchange position in the selected currency. Banks are likely to use the book base currency ledger to book the exchange gains or losses whenever the traded currency pair involves that currency. The rationale being their major economic activity is in that currency. Thus this would be in accordance with IAS21.

10. However, in the case of cross rates or currency pairs not involving the book base currency, booking the exchange gains or losses in said currency is not only non-compliance of the matching concept, it creates an open spot exchange position in a currency not involved in the trade. Whichever currency is chosen to book the exchange gains or loss, there is a profit & loss ramification because of the spot exchange positions created. Business and strategic considerations should override accounting standards. Banks are likely to choose one currency in a cross-rate, or split the gains and losses between the two currencies. Since there is exchange gains and loss ramifications, it should be Treasury management profit-driven policy, and not the call of the middle office to comply with accounting standards. IAS21 does not address this.

Don't miss out!

Visit the website below and you can sign up to receive emails whenever Pat Low publishes a new book. There's no charge and no obligation.

https://books2read.com/r/B-A-QPBY-MLUIC

BOOKS 2 READ

Connecting independent readers to independent writers.

About the Author

Pat Low clerked with Ernst & Young, Singapore, for 3 years before moving on to the banking industry where he stayed for the next three decades. He has worked in commercial banking, merchant banking and wholesale banking environments in the Singapore offices of international banks. He has managed middle and back offices with responsibilities for operations, compliance, systems, accounting, loan administration, and taxation. Pat has been involved with two start up operations and helped with systems implementation from ground up. In a dynamic industry during a growth phase, systems are challenged by the need to innovate and upgrade to support new products, regulatory and risk management demands. Pat has had hands-on experience in several in-house application developments that enhanced operational capabilities.

www.ingramcontent.com/pod-product-compliance
Lightning Source LLC
LaVergne TN
LVHW082345200926
848481LV00012B/3460

* 9 7 9 8 2 1 5 0 8 6 7 7 3 *